THE POWER OF POSITIVE HABITS

Proven Strategies *to* Exponentially Grow You

THE POWER OF POSITIVE HABITS

JON GORDON
Bestselling Author of *The Energy Bus*

Wiley

Copyright © 2026 by The Jon Gordon Companies. All rights reserved.

Published by John Wiley & Sons, Inc., Hoboken, New Jersey.

No part of this publication may be reproduced, stored in a retrieval system, or transmitted in any form or by any means, electronic, mechanical, photocopying, recording, scanning, or otherwise, except as permitted under Section 107 or 108 of the 1976 United States Copyright Act, without either the prior written permission of the Publisher, or authorization through payment of the appropriate per-copy fee to the Copyright Clearance Center, Inc., 222 Rosewood Drive, Danvers, MA 01923, (978) 750-8400, fax (978) 750-4470, or on the web at www.copyright.com. Requests to the Publisher for permission should be addressed to the Permissions Department, John Wiley & Sons, Inc., 111 River Street, Hoboken, NJ 07030, (201) 748-6011, fax (201) 748-6008, or online at http://www.wiley.com/go/permission.

The manufacturer's authorized representative according to the EU General Product Safety Regulation is Wiley-VCH GmbH, Boschstr. 12, 69469 Weinheim, Germany, e-mail: Product_Safety@wiley.com.

Trademarks: Wiley and the Wiley logo are trademarks or registered trademarks of John Wiley & Sons, Inc. and/or its affiliates in the United States and other countries and may not be used without written permission. All other trademarks are the property of their respective owners. John Wiley & Sons, Inc. is not associated with any product or vendor mentioned in this book.

Limit of Liability/Disclaimer of Warranty: While the publisher and the authors have used their best efforts in preparing this work, including a review of the content of the work, neither the publisher nor the authors make any representations or warranties with respect to the accuracy or completeness of the contents of this work and specifically disclaim all warranties, including without limitation any implied warranties of merchantability or fitness for a particular purpose. No warranty may be created or extended by sales representatives, written sales materials or promotional statements for this work. The fact that an organization, website, or product is referred to in this work as a citation and/or potential source of further information does not mean that the publisher and authors endorse the information or services the organization, website, or product may provide or recommendations it may make. This work is sold with the understanding that the publisher is not engaged in rendering professional services. The advice and strategies contained herein may not be suitable for your situation. You should consult with a specialist where appropriate. Further, readers should be aware that websites listed in this work may have changed or disappeared between when this work was written and when it is read. Neither the publisher nor authors shall be liable for any loss of profit or any other commercial damages, including but not limited to special, incidental, consequential, or other damages.

For general information on our other products and services or for technical support, please contact our Customer Care Department within the United States at (800) 762-2974, outside the United States at (317) 572-3993 or fax (317) 572-4002.

Wiley also publishes its books in a variety of electronic formats. Some content that appears in print may not be available in electronic formats. For more information about Wiley products, visit our web site at www.wiley.com.

Library of Congress Cataloging-in-Publication Data is Available:

ISBN 9781119757412 (Cloth)
ISBN 9781119757429 (ePub)
ISBN 9781119757436 (ePDF)

COVER DESIGN: WILEY
COVER IMAGE: © ABZEE/GETTY IMAGES

Printed and bound by CPI Group (UK) Ltd, Croydon CR0 4YY
C9781119757412_170326

Contents

Introduction ix

1 The Habit Before the Habit..1
2 Take a Thank-You Walk 3
3 Get Outside and Get Some Morning Sunlight....................7
4 Smile More..11
5 Create a Success Journal 13
6 Slow Down and Enjoy the Ride 15
7 Master Your Morning..17
8 Talk to Yourself, Don't Listen to Yourself 19
9 Be Your Own Greatest Encourager....................................21
10 Say Power Statements That Begin with "I Am"...............23
11 Trust in Your Big Life Plan..25
12 Pick One Word 27
13 Forgive Fast..31
14 Strengthen Your Strengths...33
15 Run Your Race 37
16 Tune Out Distractions 39
17 Lift Weights 41
18 Play Your Highlight Reel..43
19 Encourage Others..45
20 Build a Great Team...47
21 Catch People Doing Things Right.....................................51
22 Connect Before You Correct 53
23 Write Down Your Purpose Statement and Read It Each Day 55
24 Don't Let Old Battles Keep You from New Victories......57
25 Take a Walk After Meals..59
26 Get More Sleep..61
27 Squat Like a Child...63
28 Live with Integrity..67
29 Fight for the Good 69
30 Be Present at Work and Home..71

31 Turn Cash into Wealth 73
32 Be Habitually Courageous 75
33 Read More Books 77
34 Think Less (Overcome Overthinking) 79
35 Pray 83
36 See Adversity as Your Partner in Growth 87
37 Turn LOSS into a GAIN 89
38 Commit First 91
39 Be Consistent 93
40 Celebrate the Success of Others 95
41 Know Their Story 97
42 Play to Win 99
43 Don't Let Critics into Your Head 101
44 Don't Let Praise Go to Your Head 103
45 Just Show Up and Do the Work 105
46 Fear Not! 107
47 Love It! 109
48 Choose to Be Positively Contagious 113
49 Live with a Telescope and a Microscope 115
50 Focus on "Get to" Instead of "Have to" 117
51 Increase Your Positive Interaction Ratio 119
52 Drink More Water 123
53 Make Breath Work for You 125
54 Defeat Murphy 129
55 Be Humble and Hungry 131
56 Do One More 135
57 Know and Show Your Values 137
58 Focus on the Root, Not the Fruit 139
59 Shout Praise and Whisper Criticism 141
60 Don't Let the Good Get in the Way of the Great 143
61 Care More 145
62 Spend Time with Great Friends 147
63 Clear the Clutter 149
64 Commit to a Bigger Scoreboard 151
65 Love Tough 155
66 Ask Yourself Four Questions Each Day 157
67 Tell Yourself a Positive Story 159
68 Be a Giver and a Receiver 161
69 Make the Pie Bigger 165

70 Focus on Winning People Instead of Arguments 169
71 Take a Power Nap 171
72 Be Still and Be Silent 175
73 Do a Daily Dead Hang 177
74 Be a Lifelong Teacher 179
75 Reduce or Stop Drinking 181
76 Value Everyone 185
77 Elevate Your Circle 189
78 Learn from Everyone 191
79 Ask for and Receive Feedback 193
80 Eliminate the Waste 195
81 Think Intentionally 197
82 Add Play to Your Day 199
83 Seize the Moment 201
84 Create Purpose-Driven Goals 203
85 Tell Me Something Good 207
86 Slay Energy Vampires 209
87 Serve with a Caring Trademark 213
88 Implement the No Complaining Rule 217
89 Don't Waste Your Energy on Those Who Don't Get on Your Bus 221
90 Never Wrestle with a Pig 223
91 Take a Leap of Faith 225
92 Leave It Better Than You Found It 229
93 The Final Habit: Create an Amazing Funeral 231

Power of Positive Habits Resources 235
Become a Certified Positive Leader 236
Bring the Power of Positive Leadership to Your Organization 237
Other Books by Jon Gordon 238

Introduction

Several iconic books about habits have been written over the years. They taught us seven ways to be highly effective, the power of habits, and the science of how to create habits and make them stick. My goal in writing this book is not to rehash what has already been written but rather to share a collection of proven habits backed by experience and research that you can implement in your life in order to grow *you*.

At the age of 31 I was on a personal quest to become a better husband, father, man, and entrepreneur, so I began researching all the ways I could become more positive and successful. As these habits and strategies began to change my life, I knew I was meant to share them with others and started writing and sharing a weekly tip about the positive habits that were working. My quest to get better turned into a quest to help others get better—and they did.

For the past two decades, I've heard from countless people who read my newsletter and books, put these habits into practice, and saw amazing results in their lives. I believe a test of whether something is true is whether it works. If it's true, it works. If it works, it's true. Well, I can say that these habits work, and if you put them into practice, they will elevate your life.

As someone who coaches leaders, I often say that I'm not the guy who's going to teach you all the nuances on how to scale your business. Rather, I'm going to scale *you*. I'm going to grow you so you can have greater capacity, wisdom, and power to grow your business, organization, team, and family.

My promise with this book is that, as you read it and implement the habits, you will grow exponentially. And as you grow, you will become someone who exponentially grows everything and everyone connected to you. Your team, your organization, your business, and your family will all benefit because of your growth.

As you read this book, I want you to know that you don't need to implement every habit in this book to have exponential growth. Not every habit will appeal to you or apply to you. I've shared a bunch of different habits, knowing that certain ones will appeal and apply to different readers. That's why my habits include mindset habits, physical habits, leadership habits, communication habits, and relationship habits. I've found that the best habits are the ones that you will actually do and stick to and make a part of your life. Your habits decide what you do and who you become. You are the result of your habits, and the actions you take become the life that you make. So let's begin with the habit before the habit that will help you implement great habits!

1

The Habit Before the Habit

This is the habit that helps you follow through with your other habits. When you make this a part of your life you'll be more consistent in putting your habits into practice. The habit before the habit is anything you do that sets you up for success. For example, if you decide to make working out in the morning a habit, the habit before the habit would be gathering your workout clothes and sneakers the night before and putting them somewhere that is easily visible and accessible so that you get dressed as soon as you wake up in the morning. This removes resistance, moves you towards positive action, and creates momentum. Once you get dressed it will be harder to say, "I don't think I'm going to work out today," or "I have so much else to do, I'll just work out later." You will already have made a minor commitment that leads you towards the bigger commitment of working out. You can do this for any habit.

Here's another example. If you want to make reading a habit before bed, simply putting the book on your nightstand means that you'll be more likely to read the book each night. If you want to eat more healthy whole foods, food prepping on a Sunday or the night before and having the food ready in the refrigerator will make you more likely to engage in the habit of healthy eating instead of making bad choices because you're starving. Or perhaps you want to build stronger relationships with your team or customers and decide that you'll send a video message to three of them each day. The habit before the habit would be making a list of the people you will communicate with that week and that day and having it readily visible. This will make it easier and more likely that you'll take action even when you get busy and bombarded with distractions.

As you read this book and learn about the various habits you can implement, I encourage you to think about what simple habit before the habit will help you make the habit a part of your life. When you do this, you create more flow instead of resistance.

2

Take a Thank-You Walk

This habit changed my life. I was 31 years old when I lost my job and wasn't sure how I was going to pay the bills and support my family. I was filled with fear, anxiety, and stress. I was negative and miserable and made everyone around me miserable. My wife had enough of my negativity and told me that if I didn't change, we wouldn't stay married, so I'd need to change. I didn't like being miserable and wanted to stay married, so I agreed to work on myself and become more positive even in the midst of our challenging situation. It wasn't easy. After all, how do you stay positive when your life is falling apart, you don't know where your next paycheck will be coming from, you have a mortgage to pay and a family who depends on you?

I began researching ways I could be more positive. This was during the time that the field of positive psychology was emerging. I read an article that said you can't be stressed and thankful at the same time and I had an idea to start walking and practicing gratitude each day. I called it a thank-you walk, and within a week I noticed a shift in my energy and spirit. My wife noticed a change in me as well and told me to keep it up. After a month I noticed a big difference, and within a year I was becoming a different, better person in every way. I've been taking a thank-you walk for over 20 years now and it's the number-one habit that changed my life. The ideas for the books I have written have come to me during these walks. Great insights have come to me during these walks. Fear, stress, and uncertainty have been transformed into peace, faith, and calm during these walks.

So how do you do it? While walking, you simply say to yourself what you're thankful for. You can start with simple, small things like being thankful you can walk. You can say you're thankful for the ground to walk on, air to breathe, and this life that you get to live. You can say you're thankful for your health, your family, your friends, a job or business that pays the bills, or if you were jobless like I was, you can be thankful you have the means and opportunity to find a job. You can be thankful for things big and small and you can be thankful for it all. When you're doing this and feeling blessed you won't be stressed. Research shows that when you're taking a thank-you walk, you're filling your body and brain with positive emotions and endorphins that uplift you rather than the stress hormones that drain and slowly kill you.

Yes, chronic stress slowly kills you. That's why a thank-you walk is such a great habit. No matter how stressed you are at the beginning of the walk, by the end of your walk you have created a fertile mind that appreciates what you have and is ready for great things to happen. If you do this walk just one day you won't experience a huge benefit.

But if you do it daily, you'll notice incredible benefits and major life changes. Think of your mind as a garden. One day of weeding and feeding the garden doesn't make a huge difference. But if you weed and feed each day, each week, each year, the garden of your mind will become magnificent.

TAKE A THANK-YOU WALK

3

Get Outside and Get Some Morning Sunlight

I think we forget that our bodies are made up of the same organic elements found in nature. The human body primarily consists of oxygen, carbon, hydrogen, nitrogen, calcium, and phosphor, and underlying these elements are atoms (with electrons, protons, and neutrons). We mistakenly think we are physical beings when we are actually energetic beings. Just as plants need sunlight to thrive and grow, so do we. We need to spend time in the sun to power up like plants.

So instead of waking up, staying inside, and turning on the light that requires electricity, I want you to get outside and get some sun in the morning so you can electrify your body. Instead of getting on your computer or phone that must be powered up to work properly I want to encourage you to get outside in the morning and expose your energetic body to the sun so you can power up and work effectively.

According to neuroscientist Andrew Huberman, getting sunlight in the morning activates neurons in the eyes, which signals that it's daytime, which triggers a morning spike in cortisol that enhances your immune system, metabolism, and ability to focus during the day. Sunlight in the morning regulates your "circadian clock," the body's mechanism for anticipating when to wake up and when to go to sleep. This helps you wake up in the morning with more energy and wind down for a more restful night. Huberman says that morning sunlight exposure also regulates your hormones—such as cortisol, dopamine, testosterone, and estrogen—which can positively improve your mood, energy, mental health, and alertness.

Huberman recommends getting outside for at least 5 to 10 minutes on a sunny day. For even more sunlight exposure, when you have more time, take a thank-you walk, exercise, journal, or eat outside. On cloudy days you can still benefit from sunlight, but you'll want to increase your time to 15 to 20 minutes. When getting sunlight exposure, it's helpful to face the sun and look towards it, but don't look into the sun to the point that it's painful or hurts your eyes.

While this is a habit for morning sunlight exposure through the eyes, I also want to note that there are also benefits to your skin being exposed to the sun. Since we are meant to absorb the sun, like plants, it's no surprise that, according to Huberman, a study found that skin exposure to afternoon sunlight for about 30 minutes (such as by wearing shorts and short-sleeved T-shirts) increased testosterone, estrogen, mood, and libido in both men and women. To follow their protocol, get outside wearing T-shirts and shorts (hopefully, it's not too cold) for 20 to 30 minutes in the afternoon, two to three times a week minimum. Just make sure you don't get sunburned.

In a world that is spending too much time inside, the habit of getting outside and getting some sun will make a huge difference in your life. I preach this all the time to my adult children and want to preach it to you as well because I know if you try this for 30 days, you'll see and feel the difference!

4

Smile More

If you want to elevate your happiness and life, turn your frown upside down and smile more. The research is prevalent that smiling boosts your mood, happiness, health, and longevity. When you smile you produce mood-enhancing hormones and neurotransmitters such as serotonin and dopamine, which makes you feel better and lowers your stress. Since 90% of doctor visits are stress-related, by smiling and reducing your stress you're protecting and enhancing your health.

Smiling authentically also conveys confidence and creates connection. When you smile you draw people to you, and people trust you more and connect with you. Smiling is contagious, so the act of smiling also generates smiles from others, creating a more positive environment and world.

My favorite part about smiling is that when you smile at someone, you produce more serotonin in your brain and so does the recipient of your smile. Serotonin is an antidepressant, so when you smile at others you are literally dispensing antidepressants to everyone you smile at. This means that whatever job you have, you're also a pharmacist with the natural power to make yourself and the people around you feel better.

Remember, the smile has to be real for it to work. Fake smiles actually produce more stress. So think of something funny to help you smile. Smile with your eyes and your mouth. Intentionally send positive energy to people when you smile at them. Remind yourself that you are contagious and each day you can be a germ or a big dose of vitamin C.

5

Create a Success Journal

When my children were young, I read a story about US gymnast Bart Conner, who was able to overcome a torn bicep muscle to win two Olympic gold medals. When asked how he did it, he explained that when he was growing up, each night before bedtime his parents would ask him to share his success of the day. He said, "Every night I went to bed a success. Every morning, I woke up a success. When I got injured, I knew I was going to come back because I was a success every day of my life."

I thought this was such a powerful concept, so I immediately began asking my two children about their success of the day. At first my seven-year-old daughter, Jade, didn't know what a success was, so she said, "I didn't beat my brother up today." I laughed and then taught her the definition of success. Eventually she and her brother, Cole, learned to share their successes with me and it became part of our bedtime ritual.

Since that time, I've encouraged people of all ages who attended my keynotes to think about and write down their success of the day. Instead of dwelling on all the things that went wrong, all the mistakes you made and all the people who frustrated you, focus on the one great thing that happened that day, the one great conversation you had, the one event that made you smile, or the one accomplishment you're proud of.

When you write down your success each night, you're programming your mind and brain to focus on success. What you look for you will find. What you focus on shows up more in your life. If you want to test this out, start looking for red cars on the road. You'll start seeing more red cars. By thinking about your success of the day and writing it down in your success journal, you'll create and experience more success in your life. Try it for 30 days by yourself or with your family or team. If you pay attention, you'll be amazed at what happens during those 30 days. I've had countless people tell me it led to incredible achievements.

Over the years many have asked if I had a success journal they could use, and I didn't have one, so I finally created one to make it easier for you to have a place to record your daily success before going to bed. Feel free to use my *Success Journal*, or create your own with a simple blank notebook. Write down your success each night and you'll go to bed feeling like a success and wake up feeling like a success. As a result you'll have greater confidence to overcome your challenges and create the life and success you want!

6

Slow Down and Enjoy the Ride

I almost didn't see one of the most beautiful places on earth. I was busy, stressed, and had a lot on my mind. I was in Banff speaking about Positive Leadership at the Gathering, an incredible branding conference for top brands and creatives.

My family had come along with me, and my daughter said, "Dad, let's go see Lake Louise. It's amazing and beautiful."

"I don't have time to see it," I told her. "I'm preparing for my talk and have too much going on afterward and don't feel like driving the 45 minutes to see it. Besides it's just a lake and I can see pictures of it online."

After my talk, my daughter asked me again if I wanted to see the lake and I had a change of heart. It was the first time my family and I had traveled together in a while, and I decided we should go see this lake even though I didn't think it would be a big deal.

Boy, was I wrong. It wasn't just a lake, and the pictures online didn't do it justice. Lake Louise is one of the most beautiful places I've ever seen, and I'm so grateful my daughter persisted and I agreed to go.

It's a reminder to me, and hopefully to you, that in the busyness of life, which seems to be moving faster and faster, we need to slow down and make time to see the beauty all around us. We are not meant to live life indoors connected to our phones and computers 24/7. We are meant to connect with nature and enjoy places, events, and opportunities that refresh our spirit and recharge our soul.

I want to encourage you to take a break from busyness and stress. Visit a park. Take a hike. Go to a concert. Have a picnic with your family. Go see a movie in a theater. See an exhibit in a museum. Do the thing you think you're too busy to do. Create moments that make life memorable and meaningful.

As I wrote in *The Energy Bus*, the day we die we will still have emails in our inbox and calls we still have to return. We will never get it all done, so we need to slow down and enjoy the ride!

7

Master Your Morning

How you start the day is a huge factor in the kind of day you're going to have. That's why you want to make it a habit to master your morning instead of letting your morning master you. If you wake up and scroll on your phone, check your email, look at social media, and watch the news, your attitude and morning will be dictated by the news, circumstances, the urgency of others, the tone and comments on social media, and problems in the world. But if you create a morning routine filled with rock-solid rituals, instead of letting the world create you, you will create your world.

The most successful entrepreneurs, business leaders, and pro sports coaches I work with all have morning routines that they use to master their morning. To create your morning routine you can utilize various habits found in this book or come up with your own. The key is to create a routine that works best for you and that you will stick with. This routine serves as a strong foundation that allows you to withstand the storms of life swirling all around you. By creating this steady structure in the morning, you'll be prepared for the turbulence coming your way during the day.

To master your morning, I encourage you to read or listen to something positive, to think positive, and to do something positive. These three simple habits will make mastering your morning a habit and a reality. Here are a few ideas for each category:

1. **Read or listen to something positive.** Read a devotional or something that encourages you and/or listen to music or a podcast that uplifts you. My books, podcast, and DailyPositive.com are good resources for this, but of course there are many books, songs, and podcasts from others that you can utilize.

2. **Think something positive.** Practice positive thinking. Utilize many of the mindset habits in this book. Be intentional with your thoughts. Practice gratitude. Meditate. Pray. Say affirmations.

3. **Do something positive.** Take a thank-you walk. Work out. Take a yoga class. Ride your bike. Journal. Send a few messages to friends or teammates to encourage them.

8

Talk to Yourself, Don't Listen to Yourself

Just because you have a thought doesn't mean you have to believe it, especially when negative thoughts cause you to doubt and feel discouraged. Negative thoughts are often lies that will tell you things about yourself and your future that just aren't true. The key to winning the battle of your mind is first to realize that those negative thoughts are not coming from you. How do we know this? Because who would ever choose to have a negative thought? Who would choose a thought that says, "You should give up, the future is hopeless, you don't have what it takes, you aren't enough, you don't deserve this"? You would never choose those thoughts. They come into your head like bad dreams come in while you're sleeping. The truth is that your brain is an antenna and you're tuning into thoughts all the time. The negative thought pops into your head so fast you think it's your own thought. You believe it and reinforce it. Then you speak it out loud and then it does become a part of you. Then you beat yourself up for the thoughts you never chose in the first place.

To win the battle of your mind, stop believing the negative thoughts that pop into your head. After all, you are not the thoughts you think. You are the thoughts you believe and reinforce. You don't want to hang out with liars in this world, so why would you hang out with the lies in your head? Don't listen to them. Don't believe them and don't hang out with them. Instead of listening to your negative thoughts, choose to talk to yourself with positive thoughts and words.

This is truly the best advice I've ever heard and it comes from Dr. James Gills, the only person on the planet to complete six Double Ironman Triathlons—the last time at 59 years old. When asked how he did it, he explained, "I've learned to talk to myself instead of listen to myself. If I listen to myself, I hear all the reasons why I can't finish the race. I'm too tired, too old, and too sore. But if I talk to myself, I can feed myself with the words of encouragement that I need to keep on moving forward."

You can do the same. Instead of listening to the negative thoughts in your head, talk to yourself with positive words. As a person thinks, they become. The thoughts you think and the words you say become the life and reality that you create. Instead of beating yourself up, choose to lift yourself up with positive and affirming words. Speak truth to the lies and you will go through life with greater power. You will win the battle of your mind and you will win in life and in any endeavor you choose.

9

Be Your Own Greatest Encourager

As you engage in the habit of talking to yourself instead of listening to yourself, decide to talk to yourself like you would talk to your best friend. If your best friend was struggling with confidence, you wouldn't condemn them, chide them, or make them feel worse by telling them they stink and will never be successful. You would tell them you believe in them. You would cheer them on. You would remind them of their past successes and their strengths. You would share all the reasons why they will succeed. You would lift them up with your words.

This is how you should talk to yourself as well. While we need encouragement from others, we need it even more from ourselves. I want to encourage you to make it a habit to be your own greatest encourager. Don't let anyone else out-encourage you. Let your encouraging voice be more powerful and positive than any of your friends, colleagues, or family.

When doubt creeps in, trust that you have the power to overcome. When negative thoughts tell you that you won't make it, tell yourself why you will succeed. When discouragement tries to defeat you, keep encouraging yourself to win the battle of your mind and in the world. When distractions try to derail you, keep reminding yourself why your life and work matters. When your past mistakes seek to condemn you, forgive yourself and tell yourself about the positive future you're creating.

When you become your own greatest encourager, failure will not define you, adversity will not defeat you, and negativity will not sabotage you. You will win the day and the future!

10

Say Power Statements That Begin with "I Am"

A great way to talk to yourself and be your own greatest encourager is to say power statements that begin with "I am." I saw the power of this with my wife, who was the positive one in our family until two years ago when she became very negative. She kept saying, "I'm getting old. My body is breaking down. I'm sore all the time. I work out and it doesn't work. I try to lose weight and it doesn't work. I'll never be like I was when I was younger. It's pointless. I should just give up."

I said, "Honey, we can't be thinking that way. We have to stay positive."

She said, "Shut up, positive guy."

The next day I went out of town for a speaking engagement and I was gone for two days. When I got back Kathryn was all happy, positive, energetic, and bouncing around the house feeling like a million bucks. Now imagine what I'm thinking. I was home and she was negative. I go away for two days and come back and she's all happy and positive. I said, "Did you find a boyfriend or something?"

"No," she explained. "I had that Zoom call with the health coach of the company that looked at my blood, genes, and DNA." They told her she was really unique and her genes were rare—she had the genes of an Olympic athlete. So now she was walking around the house a little lighter, standing straighter and feeling more confident. "Do you want to play pickleball tomorrow?" she asked me. "I'll crush you because I am an Olympic athlete." The next day she walked around the house meal prepping for her workouts saying, "I am an Olympic athlete." Every day she worked out and ate healthier and said, "I am an Olympic athlete."

A funny thing happened. The soreness she had went away. The inflammation went down. Thankfully, she stopped complaining. She got stronger, healthier, and fitter. Two years later she looked and felt better than she had in years. What changed? Her thoughts, her beliefs, and the words she was speaking to herself.

What would happen if each day you said, *I am strong. I am healthy. I am fit. I am a world changer. I am powerful. I am a champion. I am a difference maker. I am a great teammate. I am successful. I am worthy. I am enough.* Make it habit to say, "I am _____" and watch as your confidence grows and you rise to the level of your belief. As I said earlier, the thoughts you think and the words you say become the reality you create. I hope this is sinking in.

11

Trust in Your Big Life Plan

It's big but you can't see it, and it's so great that if you could see it, you wouldn't believe it. It's your destiny and it's calling you. If you don't believe me, just remember Albert Einstein. He couldn't speak until he was four years old. He didn't read until he was seven. His parents thought he was mentally challenged. Or how about Beethoven, whose music teacher basically said, "As a composer, he is hopeless." And let's not forget Muhammad Ali, whose teacher once told him he wouldn't amount to anything. He showed her and the world that he was the greatest of all time.

The Google guys tried to sell their business to Yahoo for a few million dollars and were told to come back when they were finished with their little school project. Steve Jobs was once fired from Apple. We all know Helen Keller's story and we certainly all know our own story.

Every day we face challenges, fears, obstacles, and negativity that hit us with left jabs and right hooks. We get so caught up in the details of bills, job pressures, raising kids, fixing the house, car payments, trying to make a living, and a hundred other to-dos, that we can't even see over the piles of paper on our desk, let alone our future success.

But when times are tough and your bills are bigger than the balance in your checking account, or when your business has slowed down and you're not sure what to do next, or when your future is uncertain and everything feels hopeless, these are the times when you most need to realize that you are part of something bigger. There is greatness in you. There is a Big Life Plan for you.

Your destiny sits inside your soul like DNA sits inside your genes. You may not be able to see it but it's there, waiting to unfold if you let it. Don't let yourself get caught up in the crashing waves. Instead, jump those waves and keep your head up, looking out towards the horizon.

And if you experience a wave so big that there's no way you can jump it, then ride it. Learn from the surfer who challenges wave after wave, growing stronger, developing more balance, and becoming more skilled every day. A smooth ocean never made a skilled surfer and a struggle-free existence never made a meaningful, great life.

The next time you're facing a difficult situation, remember that there's more than what's in front of you. There is a challenge, a lesson, and a plan. Emerson said, "The wise man in the storm prays to God, not for safety from danger, but for deliverance from fear." Don't let fear get in the way of the life that is meant for you. Einstein, Beethoven, Muhammad Ali, and Helen Keller show us that anything is possible. They were real people who overcame their obstacles and doubters and discovered their greatness.

Trust that there is a plan for you and let the possibilities unfold. In the process you'll discover the great things you are born to do. You don't have to push. Just trust and your destiny will meet you when the time is right.

12

Pick One Word

Many years ago, I stopped making New Year's resolutions and started picking One Word for the upcoming year. No resolutions, no goals, just One Word that gives meaning, mission, passion, and purpose—One Word that will help me be my best.

My friends Dan Britton and Jimmy Page have been doing this for over 20 years. They originated the One Word concept and told me how every New Year's Eve they gathered with their children and each came up with a word. Then they made paintings of their words that hung in their houses to remind them to live their word for the year.

I was inspired and started doing it with my family and shared it on stage during my speaking engagements and with all my coaching and consulting clients. The transformation people experienced choosing and living their word for the year was incredible. I was amazed that such a simple concept could have such a powerful impact, but One Word sticks. While 9 out of 10 people fail with their New Year's resolution and 50% quit by the end of January, One Word is a habit most people are able to implement and maintain.

My One Word each year has had a huge impact on my life. My words over the years have been PURPOSE, SURRENDER, SERVE, PRAY, RISE, FORGIVE, STILL, CONNECTED, EXPAND, HEART, ABIDE, POWER, WHOLE, FIRST, DEPENDENCE, and BUILD. Each word has molded and shaped me to become a better person, father, husband, writer, communicator, and leader. Looking back, I know my One Word chose me more often than I chose it.

Dan, Jimmy, and I wrote a book called *One Word That Will Change Your Life*, and we've heard incredible stories of impact from countless people, schools, sports teams, and companies that have discovered the power of One Word. Several college teams put their One Words on their lockers and practice shirts. NFL and NBA teams chose their words for the season and talked about them before games. Schools made T-shirts with all their teachers' One Words. Hendrick BMW even made a One Word car! People have made One Word rocks, key chains, bracelets, and phone screen savers.

You can pick your word for the year at any time of year. I've had people learn this concept in November and pick a word to finish the year strong and then choose a new word for the new year. I can't tell you what your word should be, but I can tell you that there is a word meant for you and when you choose it and live it, your word will shape you in very positive ways.

To help you choose your word we have a three-step process that we share in *One Word That Will Change Your Life*. The first step is to look inward and ask yourself what you truly want to create this year. What do you want to achieve? What do you need to do to make that happen, or what is something that is getting in the way? As you think about these things and look within, words will start coming to you.

The second step is to look up and ask for your word to be revealed to you. I've heard countless stories of how people's words came to them. They share that the word just appeared in front of them like a neon sign or popped into their head and they knew it was their word. I know this experience well because that's how my word comes to me each year. I look in and then I look up and ask for my word. I ask and then I receive. Give it a shot. You'll be amazed at what happens.

When your word comes to you, the third step is to live your word. Make sure you choose a way to keep your One Word in front of you. Whether it's a rock you carry around with you, or a screen saver on your computer, the home screen on your phone, or some other means, you want a One Word reminder so you live your word and put it into practice. For example, the year I chose the word "Serve" I made it a practice to help people with their luggage on airplanes while traveling, and did the laundry all year to serve the family at home, and I made a pact with myself that whatever my wife asked me to do, I had to do. At the end of the year my wife said, "I've never seen you do so much for me and the kids. What's going to be your word next year?"

"Selfish," I joked. "But no, 'serve' is now a part of who I am."

I truly believe One Word will change your life if you live it each year and put this habit into practice. If you'd like my help in picking and living your word, then join me for the One Word challenge and I'll guide you through the process. Just sign up via this QR Code or use this website: onewordchallenge.com.

13

Forgive Fast

I recently drove past a sign posted on a tree near my house that said, "Forgiveness Is the Ultimate Weight Loss." It made me think about a woman at one of my keynotes who said she lost 190 pounds immediately after she chose to forgive her ex-boyfriend when the relationship ended. "Wow," I said. "That's some serious weight loss." She responded, "That's how much he weighed."

Too often we carry the weight of the wrongs someone has done to us. We hold on to the bitterness, hurt, anger, pain, and shame that weigh us down, hold us back, and make life feel heavier and harder.

Over time, this heavy energy becomes toxic and poisons our spirit, fractures our soul, and leads to discouragement and despair. One of my favorite quotes says, "Holding on to resentment and anger is like grasping hot coal with the intent of throwing it at someone else. You are the one who's getting burned."

Life is filled with many past and future moments where people will say and do things that offend you, hurt you, anger you, and cause you to hold on to the hot coal with a desire to throw it at them.

Years ago I took a trip from Florida to visit my biological father, who lived in New York, and chose to forgive him. It was after that moment of forgiveness that I was able to start writing books. Before that I couldn't write, but since then I've written over 30 books. I had to let go of the old to create the new. I had to forgive and remove the sludge from my pipelines so my purpose could flow through me.

I wish I hadn't held on to the resentment and pain for so long. I could have become a better husband, father, and writer a lot sooner. I could have grown a lot more, and grown faster.

That's why I want to encourage you to stop holding on to the coal—let go quickly and engage in the habit of forgiving fast. The faster you forgive, the sooner you'll grow!

Do an inventory of your past hurts and wrongs. Ask yourself today whom you need to forgive. Who are you still angry at? What negative experience are you still thinking about? You may not even realize that you're still angry with someone until you really think about it. Consider who or what is holding you back. Choose to forgive fast right now. The person you may need to forgive might even be yourself.

Going forward, when someone does wrong you, don't hold on to the hot coal and don't throw it at that person. Forgive fast, knowing it will help you move forward sooner and elevate your life in a greater way.

This doesn't mean you condone what they did or allow them to continue doing it, but it means you don't hold on to what they did. The person you are forgiving doesn't even have to be alive or accept your forgiveness. But by forgiving, you release yourself from the prison of your pain and past and you move forward feeling lighter, freer, and focused on creating a great future.

14

Strengthen Your Strengths

Vince Lombardi once hosted a four-day football clinic for coaches and devoted two full days to just one play, the Power Sweep. If you know football history, you know that Vince Lombardi and the Green Bay Packers won five league championships, including the first two Super Bowls, because of that one play.

Alexander the Great won his three major battles largely because of one maneuver, a right flank. In-N-Out Burger has become wildly successful and created a huge cult following with just a few menu items that they do amazingly well. Apple has made billions of dollars with just a few products that are wonderfully designed and easy to use.

In a world that says you have to provide more choices, create more products, run hundreds of plays, and be everything to everyone if you want to be successful, there is something very powerful about simplicity, clarity, and strengthening your strengths.

Before getting on stage to speak to the leaders of In-N-Out Burger, I was talking to the owner and one of the leaders of the company and made the dumb decision of asking if they would ever offer a chicken sandwich on the menu. They looked at me like I had two heads and said, "Jon, we would never do that because it would sacrifice the quality of our hamburgers. We are focused every day on making our hamburgers the best they can be." I found out that you aren't even allowed to make a hamburger unless you have worked there for a year and apprentice with one of their hamburger makers. In-N-Out knows their strengths and they focus on strengthening their strengths. You can do the same!

There are a million things you can choose to do each day, such as partake in one of the many latest-and-greatest fads, or decide to focus on one of your many weaknesses. But I want you to know that you will be at your best when you develop and strengthen your strengths.

Everyone, including Green Bay's competition, knew the Power Sweep was coming, and yet they still couldn't stop it. Coach Lombardi and his team strengthened a strength that became an unstoppable force of positive momentum, and so will you when you identify, develop, and lead with your strengths.

What are your strengths? What do you do best? What are your best attributes? What are your bestselling products? Where can you be the strongest? What do you want to become known for? Once you know the answers to these questions, spend your time, energy, focus, practice, and effort simplifying, tuning out distractions, and strengthening your strengths. The more time you spend developing your strengths, the more you'll become known for them. The stronger your strengths become, the greater the impact you'll have.

The world doesn't need another average business. The world doesn't need an average you. The world needs your *best you*. And when you strengthen your strengths you can share *your best* with the world.

15

Run Your Race

We've all heard the phrase "Comparison is the thief of joy." Unfortunately, we all compare. It's a bad habit that is wired into us. When we were kids we compared grades and who ran faster. When we were teens we compared clothes and cars. As adults we compare jobs, financial status, homes, and more. Unfortunately, we engage in the bad habit of comparing ourselves to those who look better than us, have more than us, and seem to be happier than us. With social media we do this more than ever, and we're feeling worse than ever. The more we compare, the more we despair and hate our lives.

There is a simple solution, and that is not to compare ourselves to anyone. Instead, make it a habit to go through life like a swimmer or a track runner where you don't look to the left or right but rather you look straight ahead and run your race. My friend Tim Tebow once told me on my podcast that comparing yourself to others and wanting their life means that you think you're an accident. That you were supposed to have their life but somehow you were given the wrong life. But the truth is that you are not an accident. You are given this life for a reason and you are meant to make the most of it by running your race and living it to the fullest.

Everyone's race is different. Everyone's speed and timeline are different. Everyone's hurdles and when those appear are different. The success someone has during this time should not affect where you are on your timeline. Your success might take longer and come later. Your hurdles might appear sooner in your life. Your obstacles might be greater. Your impact might look different. Their life might look better, but perhaps they just have a better video editor. You have no idea what's going on in someone else's life. But you do know what's in your heart. Don't compare and despair. Run your race with a smile on your face. This is your life, not theirs. It will unfold as it's supposed to. Make it a habit to stay in your lane, look straight ahead, jump the hurdles, and realize that life isn't meant to be a race against others. It's meant to be a journey where you develop wisdom, appreciation, character, and strength.

16

Tune Out Distractions

As I walked on the beach the other day, I noticed that certain areas were closed off by fences and signs that said, "Sea Turtle Eggs." I remembered reading that female sea turtles swim to shore between May and August to dig nests in the sand and lay their eggs. Months later, the eggs hatch and the baby turtles follow *the pure light of the moon* back to the surf.

In a perfect world, *the pure light of the moon* guides every turtle back safely to the ocean. However, as we know, we don't live in a perfect world. Sea turtle hatchlings instinctively crawl towards the brightest light. On an undeveloped beach, the brightest light is the moon. On a developed beach, the brightest light can be artificial light sources emanating from restaurants, homes, and condominiums along the coast. Unfortunately, these powerful artificial sources of light often attract the hatchlings and cause them to move in the wrong direction.

Rather than follow *the pure light of the moon* to the ocean, the sea turtles follow the wrong bright lights to a disastrous outcome. It occurred to me that we humans face a similar challenge. Rather than follow the path we are meant to follow, unfortunately we are distracted by things that move us in the wrong direction. Technology, online games, too much time on social media, bad habits, addictions, stress, busyness, and meaningless distractions lead us astray. Instead of following *the pure light* of perfection, we allow bright and shiny artificial things to sabotage our journey.

So, what about you? Are you following your priorities and pure light to the right destination, or are you allowing artificial distractions to lead you in the wrong direction? Are you following the path you were meant to follow, or are you letting meaningless things keep you from being your best?

The great news is that unlike sea turtles, you have the ability to think, adapt, and change direction when you realize you're following the wrong path. You can tune out the distractions and focus on your priorities and let *the pure light, your purpose, and mission* lead you to an ocean of possibilities and a great future!

Write down your distractions on the left side of a piece of paper. (You know what they are.) On the right side, write down your vision, mission, purpose, and things you know you need to focus on. Each day, make it a habit to focus on your vision, mission, purpose, and items of focus and tune out and eliminate the distractions that cause you to go in the wrong direction. Over time, your desire for distraction will get weaker and your mission and focus will become stronger!

17

Lift Weights

During the pandemic, I got together with a group of writers and speakers in Orange County, California. One of the guys was Ed Mylett, and when he walked into the room it was obvious that he lifted weights. He was jacked. I thought to myself, "I used to look like that." Ed inspired me to start lifting weights again and I've been consistently doing it for the past five years. Even though I'm in my 50s, I feel younger and stronger and I look better than when I was in my 30s and 40s. Even my friend Erik Spoelstra, the coach of the Miami Heat, said, "Jon you used to look like a writer. Now you look like the college athlete you were."

Lifting weights is a habit every adult should commit to. It gives you confidence and helps you lose fat, manage blood sugar levels, gain muscle, increase bone density, increase testosterone, produce human growth hormone (HGH), lower blood pressure, improve cardiovascular health, enhance longevity, and improve mental health and mood.

I work out for 30 minutes several times per week and work all major muscle groups during each session. If I work out on a Monday, I take Tuesday and Wednesday off and lift again on Thursday. Then I take Friday and Saturday off and work out on a Sunday. If I skip Sunday for some reason, then I work out the next day and keep the routine and rhythm going. Dr. Edward Phillips, associate professor of physical medicine and rehabilitation at Harvard Medical School, recommends working all major muscle groups twice a week for 30 minutes, or shorter daily sessions if you decide to work out one or two body parts per day. All health and fitness experts will tell you that any workout is better than no workout.

With that said, I believe every person should determine what kind of workout is best for them and their body and should consult with their medical practitioner before lifting weights and implementing a workout plan. To make lifting weights a habit, it helps to start working out with a certified fitness trainer in the beginning to learn how to do the exercises properly and avoid injury.

As you get comfortable with the weights and exercises, and make lifting a habit, you'll see how it enhances your mind, body, health, and mood. You'll get addicted to the feeling you get from working out, and this habit will keep you coming back for more—more strength, improved hormone levels, feel-good endorphins, power, and confidence.

18

Play Your Highlight Reel

When I was in high school I made a highlight reel of my best plays as a running back for the football team and sent it to college coaches. It not only helped me get recruited and receive scholarship offers, but it also gave me confidence each time I watched it.

You can do the same in your mind with the highlights of your life. My friend Ed Mylett came up with this idea and encouraged me to make it a daily habit. The first step is to create your highlight reel, which can include highlights from any area of your life. For example, if you want to create a family highlight reel, you can reflect on special meaningful moments with your family. Collect these moments in your mind and feel free to write them down. Then take time—five minutes or longer—visualizing these moments one after another. You can choose the camera angle and perspective. You can see yourself in the experience as if you're watching yourself in a movie, or you can watch the experience as if you're in it. As you visualize each moment, engage all your senses. Don't just watch it. Feel it. What did it feel like when you were going through it? Recall the smell. What were people saying? The more you feel it, the more real it becomes. As you play the highlight video, you'll generate the good feelings and thoughts that come from those memories.

You can create and play a highlight reel of your best presentations, sales meetings, product pitches, performances, or anything you want to reinforce in your mind. As I get ready to step on stage for a new speaking engagement, I'll often play a highlight reel of my favorite moments speaking on stage. This practice fills me with belief, excitement, confidence, and feelings that elevate my state of mind.

Most of us are already good at playing highlight reels in our mind. Unfortunately, however, we too often replay bad moments and experiences from the worst events of our life and create negative highlight reels that make us feel worse. But by intentionally creating a positive highlight reel, you can flip the script and become a positive movie director who creates a positive state of mind that elevates how you feel and think.

19

Encourage Others

Truett Cathy asked rhetorically, "How do you know if a person needs encouragement?" His response, "If they are breathing." We all need encouragement, and when you make encouraging others a habit, you'll inspire others to do more and become more than they ever thought possible.

With so much discouragement in the world and so many people telling us we can't succeed, we need to hear people telling us we can. I remember my high school English teacher telling me not to apply to Cornell University because they wouldn't accept me, and even if they did, I wouldn't be able to do the work. (It's funny that I'm a writer now.) I almost didn't apply, but a few days later I saw Ivan Goldfarb, a former teacher, in the hallway and asked him about Cornell. He said, "You apply. If you get in, then you go. You can do it. I believe in you." His words made all the difference. I applied, was accepted, and it changed my life.

Too often we think it's our role to inject a dose of "reality" into someone's life. We think it's our job to protect people from the pain of failure and defeat. We think that dreams were meant for others. I say there are enough pessimists and realists in the world. The world doesn't need more negativity and impossible thinkers. The world needs more optimists, encouragers, and inspirers. The world needs more people to speak into the hearts of others and say, "I believe in you. Follow your passion and live your purpose. If you have the desire, then you also have the power to make it happen. Keep working hard. You're improving and getting better. Keep it up. The economy is tough but you can still grow your business. The job market is not great but I believe you'll find the right job for you. We've hit a lot of obstacles but we'll get the project finished. Even if you fail, it will lead to something even better. You're learning and growing."

We all love working for and with people who bring out the best in us. We love being around people who uplift us and make us feel great. And while we'll always remember the negative people who told us we couldn't accomplish something, we will always cherish and hold a special place in our heart for those who encouraged us.

In addition to being your own greatest encourager, I want to encourage you to be an encourager of others. So often the difference between success and failure is belief. And so often that belief is instilled in us by someone who encouraged us. Leadership is a transfer of belief, so when you encourage someone, you're leading them towards a positive future.

Today, decide to be that person who instills a positive belief in someone who needs to hear your encouraging words. Uplift someone who's feeling down. Fuel your team with your positive energy. Rally others to focus on what is possible rather than what seems impossible. Share encouragement. It will help build your relationships. It matters, and we all need it.

20

Build a Great Team

No one creates success alone. We all need a team to accomplish something great. My friend John Maxwell told me "A nightmare is having a big dream with a bad team. If your dream is a 10 and your team is a 5, you're in trouble." It's essential that you build a great team and surround yourself with the right people whom you can elevate and who elevate you and your endeavors.

While I've written entire books on how to build a great team, as I thought about what to write here for this book I realized that building a great team is a habit. There are daily choices and actions you can make and take each day that will determine whether you build a great team and live the dream or build a bad team and experience a nightmare. My books *The Power of a Positive Team* and *The 7 Commitments of a Great Team* detail all the actions and commitments you can make to build a great team, but for the purpose of simplicity and what you can put into practice right now in reading this book, here are three habits to make building a great team a habit.

Recruit and attract: First and foremost, recruit and attract the right people to your team. Even in our technology-driven world, team success is all about people. Get the right people on the bus! Legendary NBA coach Pat Riley said you don't have to yell at someone who wants the same things as you do. Make sure they are a culture fit and share the same core values. Recruit people who are competent, have the right character, are committed, and can and will make the team better. The right people will do the work that causes you and your team to rise higher. The dream is possible when you have the right team.

Connect and unite: A team that is united and connected is a powerful team. A team that is divided and disconnected is a weak team. To create a connection with your team members, meet one-on-one with a team member each day. Five to 10 minutes of connecting individually with one to three people a day will go a long way in creating stronger relationships that lead to a stronger team. You also want to foster a connection among your team members by doing some of my favorite team-building exercises. Visit jongordon.com/teambuilding to learn more about them. Connection is so important because the more connected and united you are, the more committed your team will be. You'll never have commitment without connection and unity. Building a united and connected team gives you the power to achieve your dream.

Empower and develop: After you get the right people on your team, you must empower and develop them. Give them the ability to use their strengths, own their roles and responsibilities, and develop their gifts and talents so they can grow. To elevate the potential and performance of your team, you must elevate the skills and performance of your team members. It's essential that you coach, mentor, and develop them or you find a great coach to help them grow. When Zig Ziglar was asked, "What happens if we spend all this money training people and they leave?" he replied, "What if you don't train them and they stay?" When you coach, train, and empower your team members to succeed, they will make your team more powerful and successful.

21

Catch People Doing Things Right

My mentor Ken Blanchard changed the way the world leads by introducing a simple habit that produces amazing results when it is put into practice. In his iconic book *The One Minute Manager*, he encouraged us to *catch people doing things right!* This means when you see someone doing something right, recognize and praise them for it.

What you reinforce will be repeated. The research shows that the more you catch people doing things right, the more they will do the things you're praising and recognizing. This is not just a great habit for leaders and managers; it's also great for parents, coaches, teachers, and anyone who wants to help others grow and be their best. The habit of reinforcing the right actions and practices of others leads them to creating successful habits. This positive habit helps others create positive habits.

Some might ask about the practice of holding people accountable and constructively criticizing others when they're doing things wrong. Yes, it's essential that we do these things as well, but unfortunately this is what far too many focus on too often. We see what needs to be fixed and are always focused on the fixing. But the research shows that instead of always focusing on the fixing we must spend more time praising what's working.

To put this into practice you should still help people correct mistakes and point out how they can improve, but become intentional in catching people doing things *right* more often. Make this a habit and you'll see your leadership, likability, influence, and impact grow!

22

Connect Before You Correct

As a leader, team member, parent, or coach, you often have to correct team members. You must correct their mistakes, so they don't keep making them. You must correct the wrongs and make them right. But if you're always correcting without connecting, your team will see you as a problem instead of the solution.

The key to correction is to create connection first. Connect before you correct. If correction arrives before connection, you'll get burnout instead of buy-in, disengagement instead of dedication, discouragement instead of drive, and resentment instead of results.

But if you connect before you correct and your team knows you hear them, see them, are with them and for them, then you'll earn the right to correct them. They will then get better because of you. When they feel a connection, they will be more motivated to implement your correction. If your team knows you value them, care about them, and have their best interest at heart, they'll be more open to your feedback.

This is why it's imperative to invest time and energy in developing a relationship with those you lead. When you know them, you earn the right to show them how they can do things better. To put this habit into practice, implement the three-to-one ratio of connection-to-correction interactions. Try to connect three times as often as you correct. For every three interactions where you connect with a team member, give yourself permission to have one interaction where you correct them. This doesn't mean you have to connect with someone three times before you correct them. It just means that, overall, you spend three times more connecting than you do correcting. Try it for improved relationships, parenting, leadership, coaching, and teamwork.

23

Write Down Your Purpose Statement and Read It Each Day

You are not an accident. You are here for a reason and you have a purpose. Deep down you know this, and it's why *The Purpose Driven Life* by Rick Warren has sold over 100 million copies. Everyone is searching for their purpose because they know there is a purpose to be found. You wouldn't be searching for a purpose if you didn't have a purpose. I wrote a book called *The Seed* that teaches how to find your purpose. It includes making the decision to live with purpose, on purpose, and for a purpose. As you do this, your bigger purpose begins to reveal itself to you.

If you're someone who believes what I just wrote, you're on the right track. If you're someone who doesn't believe life has meaning, you can get on the purpose path right now by deciding to give it meaning. Write down a purpose statement and read it each day. When you do this and live this, you'll find more fuel for your life. We don't get burned out because of what we do. We get burned out because we forget why we do it. Purpose gives you power.

Research shows that people are most energized when they're using their strengths and gifts for a bigger purpose beyond themselves. You can fuel up with purpose each day by reading your purpose statement and then look for opportunities to live it.

Here are some examples of purpose statements:

"I'm here to raise champions."
"I make people smile and feel good about themselves."
"I help people enhance their health and happiness."
"I help my clients solve problems."
"I empower the next generation."
"I help people create a secure financial future."
"I help people create their dreams."
"I help people find and buy their dream home."
"I make my customers day, every day."
"I add value and a smile to everyone I meet."
"I bring people together."
"I make my community safer."
"I help people get better."
"I help people heal."

There are a million purpose statements you can create. I can't tell you which one is right for you, but I can tell you that when you think about your purpose and write it down, and use your strengths for a greater purpose, and decide to live with purpose and for a purpose, you'll live more intentionally and powerfully.

24

Don't Let Old Battles Keep You from New Victories

Years ago, when I was in the restaurant business, I had partners who were stealing from me. I asked to see the financials, and they refused. Afterwards, when my attorney sent them a demand letter to show me the financials, they offered to buy me out. They offered me $100,000, but I knew the value was four times that. When I countered their offer, they said take it or leave it!

I didn't want to fight and waste my energy in a legal dispute, so I took it and moved from Atlanta to Jacksonville, Florida, with my new job, my wife, and our two little children. After losing my job during the dot.com crash, I had to figure out how I was going to support my family and pay the bills.

I decided to open up a Moe's Southwest Grill franchise, which was the first in Florida. I took out a second mortgage on my home and put in the $100,000 my partners gave me and opened up the restaurant. It was a difficult, stressful time filled with many battles and much adversity. I was able to persevere and eventually opened three more restaurants, which I sold in 2005 for seven figures while my former partners' restaurant closed.

When I sold my Moe's it turned out my managing partner who oversaw the operations was not paying the bills to my produce supplier. A few months after the sale I got a bill for $80,000 worth of produce that hadn't been paid. I could have fought this and went after my managing partner but I decided to pay the bill and move on. I wanted to focus on becoming a writer and speaker. While writing that unexpected big check for the produce was painful, I knew it was the right thing to do and it freed me up mentally to pursue my mission and dream.

Twenty years later I realize that one of the key reasons why I have been able to write 33 books, travel to countless cities, speak at thousands of events, and impact millions of people is because I didn't get stuck fighting old battles. Instead, I moved forward and utilized all my energy to fight new battles and create new victories.

It's a major life lesson I want to share with you because too often we get stuck fighting old battles and then we don't have the energy or focus to fight new battles that will lead to new victories and better outcomes.

Don't waste your energy fighting battles that keep you stuck in the past. Let it go. Shake it off. Take the lesson and move on. Decide what you want to create now. Choose to move forward. Maximize your energy and focus so you can win new battles and experience new victories.

25

Take a Walk After Meals

For years I've been taking walks after meals. I didn't know why it made me feel better but I just knew it did. Now I know that it improves digestion, assists in regulating our blood sugar level, and helps us lose weight. Walking after meals has also been shown to improve heart health and enhance our mood and sleep.

When you walk after a meal, the glucose in your blood goes to support the muscles in your body that need energy to function. Walking activates the muscles, and the muscles tell your body that it needs energy. So instead of the glucose sitting in your blood, the muscles use it, thus helping to regulate and even lower your blood sugar level. Walking after a meal also burns calories, helping you to decrease fat and manage your weight.

While there's no research yet on for how long you should walk, most health experts recommend that you walk at least 5 to 15 minutes. I've found my sweet spot to be 10 to 30 minutes of walking after each meal. Usually I walk for a shorter duration after lunch and walk longer after dinner. The more you make this a habit, it becomes addictive in a good way, because you feel so much better after walking, as compared to being sedentary after a meal.

Also consider walking with a friend or family member and feel better together!

26

Get More Sleep

You can't replace sleep with a double latte. In our 24/7 fast-paced world, too many of us are doing more and sleeping less. We are recharging our phones and computers but failing to do the most essential thing that recharges our brains and bodies. Sleep is when you recharge the 100 trillion cells that make up *you*. From brain cells and blood cells to your immune system and brain function, every part of you is impacted by sleep or the lack of it.

When you sleep you build tissue, release growth hormones essential for recovery and growth, and repair muscle. Without sleep your body doesn't heal, recover, or work optimally. A lack of sleep is associated with increased risk of heart disease, stroke, diabetes, obesity, dementia, and high blood pressure. A good night's sleep optimizes how your brain functions, enhances your mood and health, and helps you maintain a healthy weight. If you want to be more alert, more focused, more attentive, more creative, and less irritable, stressed, and moody, get more sleep. If you want to be healthier, calmer, and stronger, get more sleep.

How much sleep should you get? If you make up the 1% of the population called Short Sleepers, you have a genetic mutation that requires only four to six hours of sleep per night. However, if you're like me and the other 99% of the population, sleep experts suggest you get seven to eight hours of sleep per night. The key is to find the optimal amount of time that works best for you. Sleep as much as you need in order to feel rested, energized, focused, and at your best.

To make sleep a habit, create a bedtime routine that turns your attention away from the day and towards a restful night's sleep. Limit caffeine in the afternoon and evening, engage in other positive habits such as reading before bed and listening to calm music, then breathe, pray, relax, and tell yourself *you deserve a good night's sleep.* Make your bedroom comfortable, cool, and dark—a place you look forward to going into in the evening. When you make sleep a habit and a priority, everything in your life, including *you*, will function better.

27

Squat Like a Child

Watch a toddler play. They squat effortlessly. Heels down. Chest tall. Relaxed and grounded. Then watch most adults. It doesn't look anything like that. They've lost it. The deep squat is a position the human body was designed to access daily. Losing it isn't normal. It's actually a warning sign that we need to pay attention to. In fact, many of us when in a supine position (on our back) can access the deep squat position, but when our feet hit the ground we can't do it. Why? My friend Justin Roethlingshoefer, a leading proactive health expert, says that movement or a lack of movement causes nervous system and neuroplasticity changes, for better or worse. In other words, if you move it, you keep it. If you don't use it, you lose it. If you can't get down to the ground comfortably, life starts closing in on you faster than you think. Grounded deep squats where your butt touches the ground or gets close to it is an essential movement, an exercise and habit that will ensure greater health, posture, and longevity. Cultures that maintain ground-based postures like squatting show lower rates of hip fractures, joint degeneration, and mobility loss with age. The science tells us that deep squatting enhances:

- Hip mobility and ankle dorsiflexion
- Knee health through full-range joint nutrition
- Pelvic floor function
- Spinal decompression
- Regulation of insulin sensitivity and glucose
- Circulation to the lower body

I must confess that as I wrote this book and researched key health habits, I couldn't do a deep squat. Even when holding on to a counter or chair I couldn't go all the way down. But as I practiced this habit daily, I gained more flexibility, was able to go lower and lower, and improved my balance in the process. Here's how Justin recommends we do a deep squat:

- Stand with your feet slightly wider than your hips.
- Turn your toes out slightly.
- Sit all the way down into a deep squat.
- Keep heels on the ground.
- If you can't fully squat, go as low as you can while holding on to a door frame, counter, chair, or post for balance, if needed.
- Relax into the position.
- Accumulate two minutes per day. Break it into rounds if necessary.
- Breathe slowly and deeply.
- The goal is comfort, not suffering.
- If you can't fully squat, do what you can and gradually improve each day.

From a neurological standpoint, the deep squat also grounds the nervous system, improves proprioception and balance, and maintains the ability to transition from floor to standing—a key marker of independence and longevity. If you can't squat, you borrow mobility from your future. And that's the real secret of longevity: not doing more but doing the right small habits every single day that produce big benefits over time!

28

Live with Integrity

Integrity: It's the number-one strategy to build trust and create success. It causes people to respect, listen, trust, and follow you. The word comes from the Latin adjective *integer*, which means whole and complete. When you live with integrity, you're whole and complete. There's no gap between what you say and what you do. There's no crack in your character. The foundation of who you are is strong and solid and leads to you living with power and experiencing long-term growth in your life and work.

Living with integrity means you don't sacrifice long-term success for short-term gain. It means doing the right thing when no one is watching and when it's not convenient and beneficial to you. It means you say what you'll do and you do what you say. There's no gap between who you are and what you say you are. You are the same person behind closed doors as you are on stage. You treat the janitor and the CEO the same way. You don't let circumstances cause you to abandon your principles. Rather, your principles empower you to navigate and overcome your circumstances. Doing the right thing and losing money is more important than doing the wrong thing and making money. You don't let losing games, customers, business, and opportunities cause you to lose your integrity. You live the integrity and over time you see how it strengthens, teaches, and rewards you.

The more you make living with integrity a habit, who you are and what you do become so aligned that when making tough decisions, the right decision always feels right and the wrong decision feels wrong. You'll feel it in your gut what you should do and the wrong decision won't even be an option. These decisions may not lead to short-term success but they will always lead to fortifying your foundation, which leads to your elevation and long-term growth. Living with integrity builds the trust people have in you. Like the skyscraper that requires a deep, strong foundation in order to be built for greater heights, your integrity will give you the core and strength to rise high!

29

Fight for the Good

A few weeks ago, I was playing Tim Tebow in pickleball. He's a Heisman trophy winner who is very competitive. I'm not a Heisman trophy winner but I am a Division 1 college athlete who is very competitive as well. We battled on the pickleball court, sprinting, diving, jumping, and giving everything we had. In between games we sat on the bench and talked about faith, life, and Tim's foundation that fights sex trafficking around the world. While we were talking about his foundation, he received a text from his team reporting that four girls were rescued. Then another text came in letting him know that five more girls were rescued. Then another one with more girls being rescued. In that moment it occurred to me that here is one of the most competitive people on the planet who learned how to compete on the football field and now he is competing against evil people to save lives.

I came to the conclusion that we have an innate competitive spirit and desire to compete for a reason. We innately want to compete in sports, music, dance, debate, spelling bees, and so on, so we learn to compete in order to prepare us to compete, battle, and fight for the good in this world. There's a force of evil that is always fighting against us and trying to destroy us and our children, so we have to become tougher, stronger, and smarter than our competition. We have to become more resilient and competitive than our opponent. We have to get good at fighting so we will become a powerful and positive force that fights for the good and wins the battle against evil.

Tim Tebow will tell you that his biggest impact will not come from his performance on the football field but rather the fight he is engaged in for the lives of innocent children. Yes, he wanted to beat me on the pickleball court, but that pales in comparison to his goal of beating his competition and finding new ways to rescue more children.

So, if you have a competitive spirit, don't think something is wrong with you and fight against yourself. Instead, realize that it's there for a reason and decide to use it to fight for the good. Look for ways to fight for the good in this world and you'll elevate the world and yourself in the process. Fighting on the field takes you to one level, but fighting for the good takes you to a whole other level.

30

Be Present at Work and Home

I recently asked my daughter if I traveled too much when she was growing up. I was on the road speaking a lot and was gone often. Her answer surprised me. She said, "Dad, I don't remember you being gone a lot. I remember you being home." I believe she said this because when I was home I was very present. I was engaged with my wife and kids. I wasn't on my phone a lot. I was at their games. I watched their practices. I traveled with them to tournaments. I asked them their success of the day. Prayed with them before bed. Played games with them and was very involved in their lives. When I was home I was dialed in and focused on my family. When I was on the road speaking I was present and focused on making a difference on stage for my clients. This allowed me to be successful both at work and at home.

I meet too many people who are thinking about work when they are home and feeling guilty they aren't doing work. Then when they're at work they're thinking about home and feel guilty they aren't at home. They aren't present where their feet are, and this leads to a double dose of guilt and a double dose of misery.

The solution is the simple habit of being present when you're at work and then being present when you're at home. Be where your feet are. Be fully engaged wherever you are. Give your best with the people you're with and focus on them. You'll feel good about yourself when you're at home and this will lead to greater success at work. You'll also feel good about yourself at work and this will lead you to bringing your best to those in your home. You'll be a success at work and at home, and this will elevate both your personal and your professional life. Most of all, the people who will be crying at your funeral will remember the time you spent with them.

31

Turn Cash into Wealth

You are one habit away from being wealthy. Yes, you read that right. Everyone can become wealthy because everyone can work and make money. If you can make money and make more than you spend, you can take what is left over and invest it into wealth-generating assets. You can invest in stocks, real estate, a small business, or the like. The key is to spend less than you make and make sure that when you make money, you take what's left over and make your money work for you.

There's a myth that you have to make a lot of money to become wealthy but the truth is you have to make more than you spend in order to become wealthy. I've known many people over the years who made a lot of money but never created wealth because no matter how much they made, they spent more than that. I've also known people, including my parents, who didn't make a lot of money but were able to invest their savings each year and eventually created some wealth. So it's not what you make that makes you wealthy. It's what you invest and what you invest in that creates wealth.

You turn cash into wealth by making it a habit to invest in wealth-generating assets. A wealth-generating asset is an investment that appreciates in value and/or provides a return on your investment. If you buy a stock that appreciates in value over time and you can sell it for 10 times or 100 times what you bought it for, you have successfully used cash to create wealth. If you buy a home, rent it, and make money from the rent you receive while it also appreciates in value over time, you have created wealth from cash. If you buy a small business, grow it, and can sell it for five times what you paid for it, you have put this habit into practice.

This process is not difficult, but it does require discipline, consistency, discernment, and sacrificing what you want now for what you want to create in the future. The key to making this a successful habit is to engage in the following smaller habits:

- Spend less than you make.
- Save the difference.
- Invest your savings. (Some do this weekly, monthly, or yearly. The key is to find the rhythm, opportunities, and investments that are right and best for you.)
- Repeat.

32

Be Habitually Courageous

It takes courage for an entrepreneur to start a new business. It takes courage to step into a classroom and teach a bunch of rambunctious kids. It takes courage to make decisions that are not popular but necessary. It takes courage to speak the truth when others are afraid to hear it. It takes courage to leave a job, start a new career, launch a new product, have a child, meet a group of strangers for the first time, take on a new challenge, and do what everyone, including you, is afraid to do.

Courage is a muscle. The more you use it, the stronger it gets. Courage is a choice and you can make it a habit by choosing to be courageous. You can take that step when your comfortable life says don't. You can choose the difficult path when everyone is telling you to take the easy road. You can make that call even though rejection is very likely. You can step into the battle when fear tells you to play it safe. You can speak up and speak out when the silent majority are quiet. You can do what's right when everyone around you is ignoring the wrong.

To go to the next level, you will have to be courageous in your choices and actions. As I look back on my life, I can trace everything back to being habitually courageous. Whether it was getting in a car with a suitcase and moving to Atlanta to create my life, or trying out for a bartending job when I got there, or asking the woman who would later become my wife to go out with me, or running for city council, or second-mortgaging my house to open a restaurant, or selling my restaurants to become a writer and speaker full-time, or starting Certified Positive Leader, or even choosing to write this book, I know my life is the result of being courageous. I've had a lot of friends say that what they appreciate most about me is my courage. I tell you this because I know I'm not the smartest, the most talented, or the most gifted. I can't control those things. But I can choose to exercise my courage muscle, and so can you!

The more you practice being courageous, the more courageous you will become. You'll grow your confidence, strengthen your resilience, stand out, and separate yourself from the pack. You'll elevate yourself and your future one courageous act at a time.

33

Read More Books

When you ask people what impacted their life the most, they'll tell you a person they met, an experience they had, or a book they read. The books you read have the power to change your life, but unfortunately people are scrolling more and reading less. I know this personally because I'm reading less than I used to, yet as I write this I'm making a commitment to read more.

I remember my mom giving me a copy of *The Greatest Salesman in the World* by Og Mandino, and that book made me want to write fables years later. *Illusions: The Adventures of a Reluctant Messiah* and *Jonathan Livingston Seagull* by Richard Bach changed the way I saw the world. Robert Kiyosaki's *Rich Dad Poor Dad* inspired me to become an entrepreneur and own my own business. *10x Is Easier Than 2x: How World-Class Entrepreneurs Achieve More by Doing Less* by Dan Sullivan led to me elevating and growing my business. And *Soul Keeping* by John Ortberg and *Traveling Light* by Max Lucado deeply impacted me spiritually. I know one of the reasons why I am what I am and think the way I think is because of the books that inspired, influenced, and impacted me. It's what made me want to be a writer, and I'm so grateful that my books like *The One Truth, The Carpenter, Energy Bus, Training Camp, The 7 Commitments of a Great Team*, and others are now impacting millions around the world.

To make it a habit to read more books just start with 30 minutes a day and you'll read a book every week or two. Over time, these books will impact and elevate you. And hopefully this book about habits will get you to make reading books a habit, and the books you read will shape you and your future in amazing, positive ways!

34

Think Less (Overcome Overthinking)

When are you at your best? When you're thinking or not thinking? Almost everyone will say they perform at their best when they're not thinking. When you're in the zone in a flow state, few if any thoughts are going through your mind. You are present and engaged, and the thoughts that do appear are higher level. You are knowing more than you are thinking. When you're in this state you know what to do next without having to think about it. You have incredible clarity and ultimate confidence. It's one of the best feelings in the world to be in this high state of mind where you're thinking less.

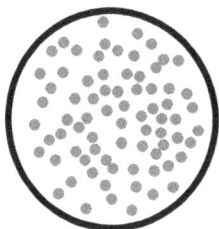 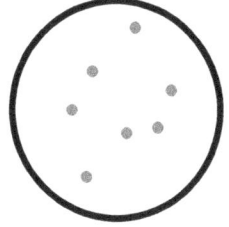

These two circles (see figure) represent our state of mind. The one on the right with a few dots represents a high state of mind that has clarity, confidence, courage, peace, and power. The one on the left with a lot of dots represents a low state of mind that has a lot of clutter, fear, worry, anxiety, doubt, and overthinking. As you look at these two circles, you're likely asking yourself how to experience a high state of mind more often, and the answer is to become and feel more connected.

The Greek root for the word *anxious* means to separate and divide. When you're disconnected, separate and divided, you feel anxious. All mental health disorders entail feeling disconnected, isolated, alone, and separate. Visualize your hands about 12 inches apart from each other with your palms facing each other. In that space and separation is where all the next thoughts flow though. Now bring your two palms together so there is no space between them. They are connected. In this connection, negative thoughts cannot flow through. The more connected you are, the fewer negative thoughts will come into your mind.

So how do you become more connected? You connect with yourself, with others, and spiritually. Start by connecting with yourself. Put away the phone, relax, breathe, close your eyes (don't do this while driving!), and just repeat one word over and over again.

Connect with others. Make time to have fun, laughter, and great conversations with friends. So many struggled with their mental health during the pandemic of 2020 because they were isolated and disconnected. But the more you connect, the healthier and happier you become.

Connecting spiritually is also essential to overcoming overthinking. As I wrote in *The One Truth*, meditation is effective because it reduces the thoughts and clutter you have in your mind. And prayer is all about connecting with your higher power, and in this connection this higher power gives you power. Think about the phrase "higher power." It implies there is a power greater than us. Well, the whole reason we don't have power and a ton of negative thoughts is because we are disconnected from this power. Remember the visual of the two hands. The more we bring our hands together and pray and connect, the more power we have and the less those negative thoughts will sabotage us. So pray more, and think less.

35

Pray

Speaking of prayer, most think of it as a religious practice, which it is, but I also like to think of it as a spiritual and metaphysical practice. The word *metaphysical* includes "meta," which means "beyond" the physical. When you pray, you're engaging in a spiritual habit that positively impacts your brain, body, and soul. Think of the soul as the integrator between the flesh and the spirit. Your soul can be governed by either the flesh or the spirit, and this is determined by whom your soul hangs out with. If it spends most of its time focused on and with the flesh—the things of this world like power, money, greed, lust, and fame—the soul will decay and disintegrate, which leads to dysfunction, discouragement, and despair. However, if your soul surrounds itself with the spirit, it renews, recharges, and integrates, which leads to healing.

When you submerge a cucumber in pickle juice and pull it out quickly, is the cucumber transformed? No. The cucumber must bathe in the pickle juice to be transformed. In this same way, our soul must bathe in the spirit to be renewed, recharged, and transformed. How does the soul bathe in the spirit? Prayer! You are spirit. Your higher power is spirit. (I personally use the term God.) When you pray, you become one spirit. The truth is you were created for connection, and every time you pray you connect with your higher power, which gives you power. That's why every time you pray, it changes you. You are never the same after you pray because when you connect with your higher and greater power, God's power becomes your power. God's love becomes your love. God's healing becomes your healing. God's creative genius becomes your next great idea.

When you continually connect with and bathe in the highest and greatest power of the universe that actually created the universe, you are going to be transformed in a positive way over time. That's why even though some might get turned off that I'm writing about God or prayer, I must share it in this book. Because if I didn't, I would be doing you a disservice by not sharing the most powerful way to elevate your state of mind and capacity to lead others. I know without a shadow of a doubt that my daily habit of prayer transformed my brain, body, and soul and increased my capacity as a leader, husband, and father. The person I am today is so different from who I was before I started to pray. In fact, my teammates from college can't believe what I'm doing now, since I was a mental wreck in college. The fact is that prayer rewired my brain from negative to positive and it reintegrated my brain and soul. The science shows it will do the same for you if you make it a habit.

In *How God Changes Your Brain*, neuroscientist Andrew Newberg shares his research that found that regular prayer and religious practice can lead to transformational beneficial changes in the brain. I had Andrew on my podcast, and while he isn't sure if he believes in God he recognizes that one's belief and practice of prayer improves focus and decision-making, boosts mood and the immune system, enhances empathy and compassion, reduces cortisol levels and stress, and leads to a feeling of oneness. Andrew found that during deep prayer, the parietal lobe, which gives us a sense of our place in space and time, can shut down and lead to feeling a stronger connection to something greater than oneself. He also found that the more you pray, the greater and more beneficial the change. I believe the science is explaining the metaphysical connection that is taking place. Oneness leads to wholeness and healing, and this leads to a better, healthier, whole you. So make it a habit to pray as part of your day!

Many don't pray because they don't know how, so it feels uncomfortable. In this spirit, pun intended, here are a few ways to pray and make prayer a part of your day:

- Wake up in the morning and just say thank you for another day. Gratitude is a form of prayer.
- If you're Christian, you can start your day with the Lord's Prayer.
- Take a walk of prayer. This is what I do almost every morning. I have a PRAYER acronym I use and share in *The One Truth*.
- When you find yourself feeling stressed during the day, stop, breathe, find stillness, and say, "I trust in you, God. I trust in your plan for my life."
- If you're a parent, pray with your kids in the morning and before bed.

- If you're married, pray with your spouse in the morning and before bed.
- Pray with friends, family, and loved ones.

36

See Adversity as Your Partner in Growth

If you've ever seen a bush that's been pruned, it may look like it's been destroyed. But the pruning isn't meant to damage it; it's meant to help it grow more fully and become all that it's meant to be. Adversity works the same way in our lives. It's not meant to destroy us but rather to help us grow. Seeing adversity as your partner in growth is a habit that will shape your perspective and life in powerful ways.

When you see adversity in this new way, you realize that challenges and struggles aren't roadblocks but essential catalysts for building strength, character, and resilience, making you better and stronger and helping you become your best self. Just as lifting weights helps you build muscle, adversity makes you build mental muscle. The adversity you face today prepares you to overcome future challenges. Your greatest obstacles are actually opportunities to develop purpose, grit, and a positive competitive advantage.

So instead of running from adversity, choose to face it, learn from it, and grow through it and because of it. When you face adversity, make it a habit to see it as your teacher designed to push you to a higher level. Don't let failure define you. Let it refine you to be who you are meant to be. Don't let the competition destroy your hope. Use it to drive you and push you to greater improvement and growth. When you experience pain, use it to find a greater purpose and know that your struggle leads to strength. Setbacks produce growth opportunities that lead to comebacks. So don't fear adversity. Make it your partner. Learn from it and use it as fuel to become stronger and more impactful.

37

Turn LOSS into a GAIN

I've lost my keys and wallet. I've lost football games and pickleball games. I've lost clients when I was in sales. I've lost my job and I've lost hope. Loss is part of life. Steve Jobs lost his job at Apple before eventually coming back and taking over the company. Walt Disney was once fired for a lack of ideas. Abraham Lincoln lost multiple elections before becoming president of the United States. And George Washington lost more battles than he won, but when he lost, he was tactical in his retreats, strategic in his thinking, and resilient in his leadership. As a result, he was able to keep the revolutionary army together and eventually win the war.

You are going to lose in life but you don't have to let loss cause you to lose your hope and future. You can turn LOSS into a GAIN by remembering that LOSS stands for Learning Opportunity, Stay Strong. When you do experience a loss, see it as a learning opportunity that will make you wiser, stronger, and better. Then stay strong, hopeful, optimistic, and respond with greater wisdom, better ideas, and new strategies in order to win. To help you do this, ask yourself the following questions when you face a LOSS:

- What I can I learn from this?
- How can I get better because of this?
- What is this teaching me?
- What actions do I need to take now?

This mindset and habit will improve your thinking, strengthen your resilience, build your optimism, and enhance your wisdom. You may not win now but when you turn your LOSS into your GAIN, you will win the future.

38

Commit First

My friend has a brother who needs a kidney transplant. My friend is a perfect match. Yet he doesn't want to give his brother one of his kidneys. He told me, "My brother is a jerk. He's never been there for me. He's never even liked me. He has never sacrificed for me. And now he only sees me as his body parts and expects that just because I'm his brother that I'm going to give him my kidney. Well, it's not happening."

As you read this you likely have an opinion about whether or not my friend is justified in his thinking. But my purpose in sharing this story is for us to look at the brother who needs the transplant. He has never sacrificed for his brother. He's never been there for him. He's never committed to him and now he wants his brother to sacrifice and commit to him. If he had committed first, I'm sure his brother would have committed in return because commitment recognizes commitment.

I meet far too many people who want their teams and family to commit to them but they haven't demonstrated commitment first. They look around and say, "That person isn't committed and so and so isn't committed." They're able to point out all the people who aren't committed but don't see the lack of commitment in themselves. I tell them you must commit first. You must lead the way.

If you want to go to the next level in your life, leadership, teamwork, and relationships, you must commit first. When you commit first and lead the way, others see and feel your commitment and will respond with their own sacrifice and commitment. The truth is that you will need the sacrifice and commitment of others in order to grow yourself, your career, your business, and more. There will be crucial moments where you'll need someone to go above and beyond for you, but how can you expect them to sacrifice and commit to you if you haven't demonstrated this commitment and sacrifice to them?

So commit first! Commit with your actions, your love, your effort, and your willingness to be there for another person. Yes, commitment will cost you. It will cost you time, energy, money, and possibly even a kidney, but commitment will come back to you when you need it most.

39

Be Consistent

A college coach I worked with told me that Nick Saban, one of the greatest college football coaches, would pull out the same brand of candy bar and eat it every day at the exact same time. He said that Saban did everything as a coach with the same kind of extreme consistency. It was in that moment that I realized that being consistent is underrated and a superpower. Saban's players didn't always like him because he wasn't always likable, but they trusted him because he was so consistent. They knew what to expect from him. They respected him. They followed him.

When you're not consistent, people don't know what to expect from you, and as a result they don't completely trust you. I remember going to speak during spring training for a Major League Baseball team and when I arrived the manager said that the players were being moody. So during my talk I told them it's not okay to be moody, explaining that if you're moody, your team doesn't know which person you're going to be that day and they'll lose trust in you. Your job is to show up every day and be consistent. So you can be your best and share your best with your teammates.

I thought they were going to be upset about what I said, but afterwards a bunch of guys told me that they needed to hear that. They realized that when you are consistent you earn the trust of others and you actually trust yourself more too, which helps you be your best.

Consistency is often considered boring by those who aren't consistent, but the results consistency creates are not boring at all. Everyone wants to do more, accomplish more, and achieve more, and consistency is the superpower that paves the way for super results. Consistency compounds! Over time, consistency creates exponential and greater success.

So make it a habit to be consistent with your mood, your mindset, your effort, your actions, your interactions with others, and your leadership. Show up and do the work. You'll earn trust in yourself and the trust of others. People will respect you, want to work with you, and follow you. It will become your superpower that powers you and your success.

40

Celebrate the Success of Others

When I started out as an author I was jealous of the success of others. Why wasn't my book a bestseller? How come they were speaking on the big stages and I wasn't? Why couldn't my book be a huge hit? One of the people I was jealous of was Patrick Lencioni, who wrote the *6 Types of Working Genius: A Better Way to Understand Your Gifts, Your Frustrations, and Your Team*, which is a genius concept. Rather than celebrating his success I was jealous of his success and impact. Then one day I realized how miserable I was because I was jealous and resentful. I made a decision right then and there that I was going to celebrate his success and impact. I was going to root for him and respect him, not resent what he was accomplishing.

A funny thing happened. As I celebrated Pat and the success of others, I started to experience more success of my own. As I celebrated others, I also envisioned my own success. Instead of resentment I felt hope, optimism, and excitement about what I was creating. By transforming how I looked at the success of others, I created a mindset that was focused on success rather than the lack of success. I worked harder, felt lighter and freer, and believed more. A few years later, after five years of being released, my book *The Energy Bus* hit number one on *The Wall Street Journal* business bestseller list. Out of the blue I received an email from—guess who?—Patrick Lencioni, encouraging me and celebrating the fact that my book was a number-one bestseller. Since then we have become great friends and have done events together where we celebrate each other and make a greater impact together.

I have made it a habit ever since to celebrate the success of others, and I encourage you to do the same. You'll create the energy that matches the success that you want. Instead of living in lack, you will attract and experience more success.

41

Know Their Story

Johnny was known as the annoying guy who hung around the waiting area of the Hendrick Auto Lexus dealership in Charlotte and bothered the employees. After receiving a number of complaints about him, Steve Strickland, the new general manager, invited Johnny into his office. He found out what his employees already knew. Johnny wasn't there to buy a car. He just wanted to have conversations and talk to people.

Steve learned that Johnny had worked in one of the towers of the World Trade Center but he wasn't there on 9/11 because he had a doctor's appointment. Many of his friends died that day, so Johnny and his wife moved to Charlotte for a fresh start.

One day Johnny brought his car to the dealership to get serviced and liked the coffee and the atmosphere so much he came back to hang out. Steve told me that in listening to Johnny's story he realized that Johnny wasn't looking to bother anyone. He was looking for a family. Instead of telling Johnny to get lost and stay away from the dealership, Steve actually hired him to be part of their customer service team.

At first the employees weren't happy with Steve's decision. But the more they worked with Johnny and learned his story, the more they grew to love and appreciate him. He's become so popular and indispensable to the team and the dealership that he's now known as Johnny Lexus. No one even knows his real last name. Everyone just calls him Johnny Lexus.

Johnny Lexus has gone from the guy no one wanted at the dealership to a beloved team member who represents the business's brand—all because Steve Strickland took the time to hear Johnny's story.

It's a great lesson for all of us. Everyone we work with and everyone we meet has a story to tell. I've learned that amazing things happen when we get to know their story. If you're a leader or member of a team, remember that everyone you work with is bringing their story to work. Your job is to get to know their story, and when you do you will know them a lot better. When you know them better, you will be less likely to see them as annoying, difficult, or negative and more likely to see them as someone who's searching to belong, to matter, and to add value.

Steve took the time to listen and hear Johnny's story. Johnny Lexus is now living a better story.

42

Play to Win

There was a time in most of our lives when we had no fear—that feeling when we jumped from the jungle gym and slammed our little bodies to the ground. Perhaps it was when we went on our first rollercoaster, or when we were in high school and felt that there was nothing we couldn't do. No goal was unattainable. We were an unstoppable force that would think of something and then make it happen. Then, as time goes by, the world tells us more frequently that we can't do what we want. The doubters laugh at our goals and try to persuade us from going after our dreams.

They say, "You're crazy. It's too hard. Why don't you do this instead? You should play it safe." They act as if dreams were meant for others but not people like us. They surround us with negative energy and try to instill their own fears and insecurities in us. We not only begin to know the word "fear," but we start to understand what it's like to be fearful. With so many people telling us we can't do something and so few telling us we can, it's hard not to let fear into our lives. Unfortunately, this is how many of us go through life.

Whether we're 20 or 50, many of us become so scared of losing what we have that we don't go after what we truly want. We play it safe and hold on so tight to the status quo that we never experience what could be. We believe the doubters and don't take chances that will move us one step towards our dreams. I call this "playing to lose."

We see this in sports all the time when a team has the lead. They start to think about how not to lose instead of how to win. They hold on so tight to their lead that they start playing safe and scared. You can see it in their energy and body language. As a result, the other team takes chances, plays with no fear, and eventually gains the momentum and wins.

To live a life filled with positive energy, we must learn to repel the energy of fear. Whether it comes from within or from another person, we must overcome fear and adopt a "play to win" mindset. Playing to win requires a commitment to yourself that even if you fail, you will never give up and never let your goals and dreams die.

Those who play to win know that success is not given to us. It is pursued with all the energy and sweat we can muster. Obstacles and struggles are part of life and only serve to make us appreciate our success. If everything came easy, we wouldn't know what it felt like to truly succeed. Obstacles are meant to be overcome. Fear is meant to be conquered. Success is meant to be achieved. They are all part of the game of life, and the people who succeed habitually play to win and never give up until the game is over.

43

Don't Let Critics into Your Head

In our modern social media–driven world, you'll have more fans and more critics than ever. When I started speaking, I had a friend who knew an event planner who booked speakers. I asked him to connect us and she agreed to come to one of my talks. After my talk she told my friend that I wasn't any good and I wasn't going to make it. She suggested that if I was stubborn and wanted to stay with it, I should get coaching from a speaker and coach she knew.

When my friend told me what she said, I was crushed. I thought about giving up. I realized I wasn't very good. But then I asked, "Who's good when they're first getting started?" As an athlete I had been benched, cut from a team, and told I wasn't good enough, but each time I had worked hard, overcome setbacks, and risen above. I'm stubborn and didn't want to fail at something I felt I was meant to do, so just like I had done as an athlete growing up, I committed to getting better. Thousands of talks and years later I realize that my mission, dedication, and action were more powerful than her negative opinion.

Don't let critics into your head. Be so invested in your craft that you don't have time to listen to the naysayers. No time for negativity. You're too busy creating your life. After all, critics write words but they don't write the future. You do with your positive action. History doesn't remember the critic; it remembers the one who withstood criticism to accomplish something great. The critics love to tell you why you won't succeed, and your job is to simply do the work and succeed. Not to prove them wrong but to prove yourself right. Never let the opinion of others define you and your future. Your work, leadership, and mission are too important to allow others to define your destiny.

44

Don't Let Praise Go to Your Head

In addition to not letting critics into your head, you also don't want to let praise go to your head. Praise feels good but it can also make you arrogant and overconfident if you focus on it too much. Even worse, you can allow this praise to define you and your identity. So, when you're receiving praise, you feel great about yourself and your life. But when you aren't receiving praise you feel empty and crave it. Like a drug, you'll feel great when you have it, and when it runs out you'll go into withdrawal and do anything to get more of it. You'll become a praise addict and your worthiness and happiness will always be determined by the approval and praise of others. When this happens, praise can become more dangerous than listening to criticism.

That's why I say don't let praise go to your head. Receive it, be thankful for it, know that it doesn't define you, and get back to work. Words of another, good or bad, do not define you. You are defined by who you are on the inside. You are defined by your essence. You are defined by knowing who you truly are. You are made in the image of the Creator of the universe. When you know this, no one can make you or shake you. Criticism can't defeat you and praise won't entice you. You are here to do your work and live your mission and purpose, and that is more than enough.

45

Just Show Up and Do the Work

If they praise you, show up and do the work.

If they criticize you, show up and do the work.

If no one even notices you, just show up and do the work.

Just keep showing up, doing the work, and leading the way.

Lead with passion.

Fuel up with optimism.

Have faith.

Power up with love.

Maintain hope.

Be stubborn.

Fight the good fight.

Refuse to give up.

Ignore the critics.

Believe in the impossible.

Show up.

Do the work.

You'll be glad you did.

46

Fear Not!

There's a storm headed your way. Fear not!
You'll likely lose power. Fear not!
You're not sure what the future holds. Fear not!
You're not sure how the meeting went. Fear not!
You're waiting on the medical report. Fear not!
You're getting ready for the big game. Fear not!
You might lose your job. Fear not!
You don't know what college you will go to. Fear not!
Your parents are getting a divorce. Fear not!
You don't think the interview went well. Fear not!
They're putting a lot of pressure on you. Fear not!
You may not hit your numbers. Fear not!
There's a lot of chaos in the world. Fear not!

Fear not doesn't mean you take reckless action.

Fear not doesn't mean you ignore the reality of the situation.

Fear not doesn't mean you make stupid decisions.

Fear not doesn't mean you don't prepare.

Fear not doesn't mean you don't care.

Fear not doesn't mean you don't feel fear.

Fear not means you let go and know you're not in control.

Fear not means you don't let fear consume you.

Fear not means you don't let fear guide you.

Fear not means you don't let fear paralyze you.

Fear not means you don't let fear sabotage your health.

Fear not means you won't let fear steal your future.

Fear not means your trust is greater than your fear.

Fear not means you move forward with faith.

Fear not means you have hope today.

Fear not means you still dream about tomorrow.

Fear not means you believe that the best is yet to come.

47

Love It!

I sat for a while staring at the computer screen. I couldn't write. Not even a sentence. It had been a week since I'd started to write a new book but I had nothing. Each December I write a new book and it usually flows well, but not this time. This time I was filled with fear.

Fear that I would disappoint the people who enjoyed my other books. Fear that I couldn't live up to the success of *The Energy Bus*. Fear that people would say my best writing was behind me. Fear that I would write a piece of junk. I knew I had to conquer this fear, and in that moment I was filled with thoughts that not only would help me overcome my fears but would also become a significant lesson in the book I was writing, *The Carpenter*.

I realized the antidote to fear is love. So instead of the fear of failing, I decided to focus on my love of writing, my love for the reader, and my desire to make a difference. From that moment on, the book flowed. I wrote it in two and a half weeks and discovered that if you focus on love, you will cast out fear.

Today I want to encourage you to do the same and build your life, work, business, school, project, and team with love instead of fear. Remind yourself that if you aren't building it with love, it won't become all that it can be. Only through love will you create something special, magnificent, and compelling. Only through love will you build a masterpiece.

So if you're trying to build a business, focus on the love you have of building it rather than the fear of losing it. If you work at a school, focus on loving your students instead of fearing all the new testing standards. If you're a young athlete, dancer, musician or artist, focus on your love of playing and performing and creating instead of your fear of failing. Worrying about the outcome and what people think will steal your joy and sabotage your success, but loving and appreciating the moment will energize you and enhance your performance.

And if you're a coach or manager building a team, remember that whatever you try to build with fear will eventually crumble, but that which is built with love will endure. If you build your team with love, they will become more and do more than you ever thought possible.

Most of all, as you build with love, know that you will face many challenges and negative forces that can shift your focus back to fear if you let it. When this happens, decide to *love all of it*. When you love all of it, you will fear none of it.

Love the struggle because it makes you appreciate your accomplishments.

Love challenges because they make you stronger.

Love competition because it makes you better.

Love negative people because they make you more positive.

Love those who have hurt you because they teach you forgiveness.

Love fear because it makes you courageous.

The secret to life and the greatest success strategy of all is to *love* it.

48

Choose to Be Positively Contagious

The flu is not the only thing you catch at work. Turns out you are just as likely to catch someone's bad mood and negative attitude. Yes, the latest research demonstrates what we've all known to be true: Emotions are contagious. Researchers call them emotional contagions and they impact our work environments, productivity, teamwork, service, and performance in significant and profound ways.

As we know all too well, one negative employee can pollute an entire team and create a toxic work environment. One negative leader can make work miserable for their team. An employee in a bad mood can scare away countless customers. Complaining can act like a cancer and spread throughout the entire organization and eventually destroy your vision and goals. And pervasive negative attitudes can sabotage the morale and performance of teams with great talent and potential.

That's the bad news, but there's also good news.

Positive emotions are just as contagious as negative emotions. One positive leader can rally a group of willing people to accomplish amazing things. One chief energy officer who sits at the welcome desk can positively infect every person who walks into your business, school or workplace. One positive team member can slowly but surely improve the mood and morale of their team. And pervasive positive attitudes and emotions at work can fuel the productivity and performance of your organization.

Emotional contagions are the reason that, when I speak to businesses, schools, and sports teams, I say that you are not just a creation of your culture but rather that you are creating it every day through your thoughts, beliefs, and actions. What you think matters. How you feel matters. And the energy you share with others really matters.

Every day you have a choice. You can infect others with a negative attitude or affect them with your positive energy. Your attitude is contagious and I want to encourage you to make it habit to share positive contagious energy at work and at home. Show up each day with enthusiasm. Maintain a positive attitude. Energize the people you work with. When you are positively contagious, you uplift everyone and you rise higher!

49

Live with a Telescope and a Microscope

Almost every writer, speaker, and performance coach shares the importance of having a vision for your future. A vision is supposed to be energizing and exciting. But the other day it hit me that sometimes a vision doesn't energize you. Sometimes it depresses you because it seems far away and impossible to achieve. In these moments, it's important to remember that just because you have a vision doesn't mean it's meant to happen now. Your vision is meant to show you what's possible for your future.

Don't let it frustrate you. Let it fill you with possibility and passion. If you see it, you can create it. If you have a vision, know that you also have the power to make it happen. The key is to just keep moving forward with grit and optimism towards your vision one step at a time.

To help you do this, you'll want to go through life with a telescope and a microscope. You need both. The telescope allows you to see the big picture. The microscope helps you zoom-focus on what you need to do today to realize the big picture in the telescope. With only a telescope and no microscope, you have vision without execution, which leads to nothing. If you have a microscope without a telescope, you'd likely lose sight of the big picture and get frustrated by all the challenges of today. Together, the telescope and microscope provide you with the right combination of inspiration and action to create your future. The journey isn't easy, but living with a telescope and a microscope each day will allow you to see where you're going, remember why you're going there, and know what steps you need to take today.

50

Focus on "Get to" Instead of "Have to"

Who knew that two simple words could change your mindset, your perspective, and your approach to work and life? Just two words have the potential to enhance joy, productivity, and performance and transform a complaining voice into an appreciative heart.

So often we say things like "I have to take the kids to practice." "I have to go to this meeting." "I have to finish this project." "I have to go to work today." "I have to take care of this customer." "I have to share this new information with my team." "I have to attend that event."

We act as if we don't have a choice, as if we're imprisoned by a paycheck and the expectations of a world that forces us to do things we don't want to do. But in reality we do have a choice. We can choose our attitude and our actions. We can choose how we view our life and work. We can realize that every day is a gift. It's not about what we *have* to do. It's about what we *get* to do.

We get to live this life while so many others—like my mom, who passed away at 59—leave this world far too early. We get to drive in traffic while so many are too sick to drive a car or can't afford one. We get to go to a job while so many are unemployed. We get to raise our children even if they drive us nuts at times! We get to interact with our employees and customers and make a difference in their life. We get to use our gifts and talents to make a product or provide a service. We get to eat three meals a day while millions of people are starving. We get to work on projects, answer phone calls, serve customers, participate in meetings, design, create, share, sell, lead, and suit up every day for the game of life.

When you make it a habit to focus on "get to" each day, you'll feel grateful instead of stressed. So when you're feeling thankful and focusing on "get to," you fuel up with the positive emotions that uplift you just like I shared in Take a Thank-You Walk. People who do this report feeling more energized, productive, and engaged at work and at home.

Sure, there'll be challenges and life isn't easy, but if you approach each day with a "get to" mindset, you'll live a more meaningful and powerful life. So today, join me in saying, "My life is a gift, not an obligation, and I *get to* make the most of it."

51

Increase Your Positive Interaction Ratio

Psychologist John Gottman's pioneering research found that marriages are much more likely to succeed when the couple experiences a five-to-one ratio of positive-to-negative interactions, whereas when the ratio approaches one-to-one, marriages are more likely to end in divorce. Additional research also shows that workgroups with positive-to-negative interaction ratios greater than three-to-one are significantly more productive than teams that do not reach this ratio.

So what does this mean for you and me? For most of us it means we need to increase the number of positive interactions we have at home and at work and reduce our negative interactions. We need to engage each other with more smiles, kind words, encouragement, gratitude, meaningful conversations, honest dialogues, and sincere positive interactions. And to foster these actions we need to create personal and team rituals that help us interact more positively. If we turn them into individual habits that are part of our organizational process, they are more likely to happen.

For instance, at home you might decide to take a walk with your spouse each night after dinner and talk about the positive things that happened at work. The more you practice this, the more it will become ingrained in your life. At work you might make it a point to intentionally connect in a positive way with three people each day. As a manager, you can spend more time praising your employees for the things they do right rather than always focusing on what everyone is doing wrong. A manager I know makes it a point to personally praise five people every week. As an organization you might gather all of your employees on a call once a day to share a positive message. Or perhaps you might gather your sales team together each week and have team members share success stories. The ideas are infinite. The key is to intentionally cultivate more positive interactions to fuel success.

However, please know that this doesn't mean we should never have negative interactions. Barbara Fredrickson's research from the University of Michigan shows that if a work group in a company experiences a positive-to-negative interaction ratio of 13-to-1, the work group will be less effective. This implies that no one is willing to confront the real problems and challenges that are holding them back.

Sometimes we need to confront a situation to move past it and, as we know, ignoring problems that stare us in the face doesn't work. Negative interactions (I like to use the term *growth* instead of negative) are necessary as long as they occur much less frequently than positive interactions.

Positive interactions are essential to a healthy marriage, positive work environment, and individual and team success. In this spirit, when you're finished reading this, I encourage you to go thank someone at work or at home and let them know how they impacted your life in a positive way. Then make it a habit!

52

Drink More Water

In a world of energy drinks and caffeinated beverages, water is the ultimate energy drink. Research shows that a lack of water consumption leads to fatigue and headaches. Unfortunately, most of us are walking around dehydrated without realizing it. Even a small decrease in your weight causes a significant drop in your energy level. The human body is made up of about 70% water, not Diet Coke or double lattes (ha-ha). So water is the fuel source you need for increased energy, enhanced health, and optimized bodily function.

Every one of your body's processes is enhanced with proper hydration. Digestion improves, your metabolism increases, and your blood flows easier. Think of water as the oil your engine needs to make everything run properly. If the warning light on the dashboard of your car comes on to let you know your oil is low, you would immediately add more oil to your car to make sure you don't destroy your engine. Yet many of us are walking around living with a warning light that we need to fill up with more water and we're ignoring the signal. If you want to be your best and have more energy and clarity, the key is to act as if the warning light is on every day and fill up with more water.

So how much water should we drink? While we've all heard the eight cups of water per day rule, this is actually a myth. Each person requires different amounts of water, based on their weight and activity levels. To determine how much water you need, take half of your body weight and drink that number of ounces in water. Thus a 100-pound person would drink 50 ounces of water a day to stay hydrated. Those who exercise must drink even more water, depending on how much you perspire during your workouts.

53

Make Breath Work for You

Breathwork is the most primitive behavior we have. Before language, before strategy, before effort, there was breath. We take our first breath when we're born and our last one when we leave this world. In a culture obsessed with doing more, breathing well is often the most overlooked habit for health and healing.

As my friend Justin Roethlingshoefer, one of the leading experts in proactive health and author of *Holy Health: Waking Truth for a Sleeping World*, teaches: "Change the breath, and you change the state of the body, the mind, and the spirit." He explains that breath is not passive. When you actively change your breath, you can speed yourself up or slow yourself down. You can induce anxiety or resolve it. You can become frantic or focused; you can disconnect or come home to yourself. Breathwork is foundational to peace, presence, and connection because it's the fastest way to communicate safety to the nervous system. It is the body's built-in whisper you can use to transform "I am scared and unsafe" into "I'm safe and ready for what's next." Physiologically, breathwork:

- Increases VO_2 max (the maximum oxygen a body can use during intense exercise) by improving oxygen uptake and efficiency
- Improves oxygen delivery to the brain, sharpening mental clarity and focus
- Regulates the nervous system, reducing anxiety and depressive symptoms
- Lowers inflammation and stress hormones
- Creates coherence between heart, brain, and body

Spiritually, breathwork restores awareness. When breath becomes intentional, connection is restored to God, to yourself, and to others. In busy seasons, breathwork keeps you grounded. In anxious moments, it brings you back to center. In leadership, it preserves clarity and restraint. In prayer, it creates space to hear the whisper.

- Make breathwork a habit.
- Make breath work for you.
- Enhance your breath.
- Raise your state of mind.
- Elevate the trajectory of your life!

Justin recommends this simple breathwork exercise:

1. The physiological sigh (for immediate calm)

This is the fastest way to reduce anxiety and stress.

- Inhale two times through the nose (belly fill first then the chest).
- Exhale slowly through the mouth.

- Repeat 10–20 times.
- Finish with a breath hold for 60 seconds.

Use this when you feel overwhelmed, anxious, or reactive.

2. Box breathing (for focus and leadership)

This restores control and mental clarity.

- Inhale through the nose for 4 seconds.
- Hold for 4 seconds.
- Exhale through the nose for 4 seconds.
- Hold for 4 seconds.
- Repeat for 3 minutes.

Use this before difficult conversations or decision-making.

3. Resonant breathing (for daily regulation and peace)

This builds long-term nervous system balance.

- Inhale through the nose for 5 seconds.
- Exhale through the nose for 5 seconds.
- Breathe slowly and quietly.
- Continue for 5 minutes.

Use this in the morning, before bed, or during prayer to restore alignment.

54

Defeat Murphy

You've heard of Murphy's Law, right? Whatever can go wrong will go wrong—and usually at the worst possible time. Unfortunately, Murphy's Law seems to play out all too often, and when a series of bad things happen to you it can lead you to expect more bad things to happen. Instead of hoping for the best, you start to expect the worst and act accordingly.

Gus Bradley, a longtime NFL coach, told me about a great way he helps his team deal with negative events (a crucial interception, penalty, injury, bad weather, etc.) and avoid the victim mindset that can accompany them. During training camp, Gus tells his team about this fictional guy Murphy whom the law is named after. Murphy is a big jerk who wants to ruin their practice, games, and season. He says that Murphy often shows up at the worst possible time. But instead of being scared of Murphy, they are going to tackle him when they find him.

They expect to see Murphy, and when they do they have an even greater expectation that they will defeat him. Instead of a victim mindset, they have a hero mindset. They expect the battle and they believe they will win the battle. You can do the same. Life is filled with challenging circumstances, but you can rise above them. Life is hard but you are strong. The struggle is real but so is your ability to overcome it. Strength, character, and mental toughness don't arise from easy circumstances. I've never met a great leader with an easy life. When the world becomes harder, you can become stronger. Murphy is tough but you are tougher.

55

Be Humble and Hungry

Years ago while speaking at a leadership conference in Dallas, I looked over to the left and saw Zig Ziglar sitting there in the front row. Zig was the iconic, legendary speaker who impacted millions of lives and careers. He's famous for saying, "If you help enough people get what they want, you'll get what you want," and "Some people are so good at complaining you'd think they were getting paid for it," and "I'll see you at the top." I ran over to him and said, "Zig, I can't believe you're here. One of my goals in life was to meet you."

He replied, "You need to have bigger goals." He was still sharp and funny after all these years. While I was speaking I noticed he was taking notes. It wasn't because I was on stage; anyone could have been on stage and he would have taken notes. At 82 years old he was a lifelong learner, and still humble and hungry after all these years. He only lived a few years after that but the lesson he taught me lives on. Whether you're just starting out and trying to make a name for yourself or you have achieved the pinnacle of success, it's important to remember to be humble and hungry. These two words are the key to a life and career of continuous improvement and growth.

Be Humble

- Don't think you know it all. See yourself as a lifelong learner who is always seeking ways to learn, grow, and improve.
- See everyone as a teacher and learn from everyone you meet.
- Be open to new ideas and strategies to move your life and work to the next level.
- Live with humility because the minute you think you've arrived at the door of greatness, it will get shut in your face.
- As C. S. Lewis said, "Humility doesn't mean you think less of yourself. It just means you think of yourself less."
- Realize there is no finish line. Keep growing till the end.

Be Hungry

- Have a great desire to continuously learn, improve, grow, and dream.
- Seek out new ideas, new strategies, and new ways to push yourself out of your comfort zone.
- Invest the time, energy, sweat, and dedication to be your best.
- Be willing to pay the price that greatness requires. Don't be average. Strive to be great.
- Become the hardest worker you know.
- Make your life and work a quest for excellence. Every day ask yourself, "How I can be better today than I was yesterday?"
- Make your next work your best work.

As I share this advice, my hope is that you'll make these two words a habit. Regardless of your age, education, or career status, if you stay *humble and hungry,* I'll see you at the top!

56

Do One More

In 2004 George Boiardi was hit in the chest with a lacrosse ball and died on the field. He was the selfless, hardworking, committed captain of the Cornell lacrosse team who jumped in front of a shot as he tried to prevent the opposing team from scoring a goal. A few days after his death, his teammates gathered in the locker room. They were devastated, discouraged, and in despair, and had a decision to make. Were they going to end their season, or continue playing? They decided to keep playing. But they didn't want to make their season about winning for George. Rather, they wanted to honor him by playing like he did. He was the hardest-working, most loyal, selfless teammate they had ever had and they were committed to being like him.

That team would go on to overcome all odds, outperform their talent, surprise everyone in the lacrosse world, and make it to the postseason tournament. George wore the number 21 on his jersey and I wrote about him, his teammates, and that season in the book *The Hard Hat: 21 Ways to Be a Great Teammate*. Years later Rob Pannell, one of the greatest lacrosse players of all time, who never met George, was so influenced by him that he made a decision as a Cornell lacrosse player he was going to do "one more" for George. To Rob, 20 was normal; 21 meant going above and beyond and sacrificing by doing one more than normal. When the team did sprints, he did one more. When they lifted in the gym, he did one more. When doing a timed exercise, he did one more minute or one more second than what was expected. He always did one more and it drove his performance and led to an incredible college and pro Hall of Fame career.

I want to encourage you to make it a habit to do one more in all that you do. Give a little extra. Do more than what's expected. Try one more time. Make one more phone call. Do one more rep. Help one more team member. Thank one more person. Write one more page. Run one more minute. Come up with one more idea. Give up what's easy in order to do what's harder. Over time, one more becomes a lot more success.

Amazingly, the 2025 Cornell lacrosse team won a National Championship 21 years after George Boiardi's death by becoming the kind of teammates George was. They truly lived and embodied the 21 ways to be a great teammate and became a great team by sacrificing for each other and doing more than what was expected. Cornell's head coach wore a hat with the number 21. Fans in the stands wore 21 shirts. It was clear something special happened, and I believe special things will happen in your life when you decide to sacrifice what's normal and commit to doing one more.

57

Know and Show Your Values

The culture of your family, school, organization, and team will determine how they perform, compete, and thrive in a challenging world. Culture is a competitive advantage. When you create a great culture, it drives the talent your people have towards greatness. Schools with great cultures have students who perform at a higher level. Businesses with a great culture outperform companies with a bad culture. Families that focus on their culture provide kids with confidence to create their future.

You also have a culture within you. You are a culture of one and your culture is created by knowing your values and showing your values. Knowing your values is knowing what you stand for, what matters most to you, and what you would want others to say about you.

Showing your values is putting them into practice and living them. It's seeing the values you write down on a piece of paper and also seeing them displayed in how you live, work, and show up for others. If one of your values is service but you don't take the time to serve, then you aren't living that value. When you don't live the values you say are important, you become weak and powerless.

When you live your values and they consistently show up in your life, you become powerful and strong. Knowing and showing your values is a habit that will cause you to rise to a higher level in all that you do.

Many often make this complicated. It doesn't have to be. Know what you stand for and stand for what you value. Know it. Show it. Do this often. Make it a habit. Your internal culture becomes stronger and the impact you have on your team and organization becomes greater.

58

Focus on the Root, Not the Fruit

We live in a world that loves to focus on the fruit of the tree: the wins and losses, numbers, stock prices, KPIs, test scores, and so on. We focus so much on the outcomes and the fruit of the tree that too often we ignore the root. When you focus on the fruit and ignore the root, the tree dies. Unfortunately, most people and organizations don't realize that the tree is dying until it's too late.

The truth is that if you want great fruit, you must make it a habit to focus on the root. The root of the tree is your culture, people, mission, purpose, values, essence, and core of who you are and why you do what you do. Habitually focusing on and investing in the root doesn't mean you don't look at the numbers and measure your outcomes and success. Actually, it's essential to measure the fruit. But you do so knowing that your fruit is just a byproduct of how well you invest in your root. Measuring your fruit will help you gauge where you need to invest more in the root. When you invest in the root by developing your culture and people and focusing on the mission and values and make them a priority, you'll get a great supply of fruit.

As you invest in the root, keep in mind that there will be times it takes a while for the fruit to show up. Sometimes life is like a bamboo tree where it takes years of water and nurturing before you see the sudden and amazing growth. Don't let the lack of fruit discourage you. Keep investing in the root, keep improving your tactics and skills, and trust that a harvest is coming.

59

Shout Praise and Whisper Criticism

These habits come from the original Olympic Dream Team and Detroit Pistons coaches Chuck Daly and Brendan Suhr. They won NBA Championships and an Olympic Gold medal with a lot of talent and great communication. They gained the trust of their players and built winning teams by praising in public and constructively criticizing in private. Shouting praise means you recognize someone in front of others, and whispering criticism means you coach them in private to get better. Both build better people and teams.

Shouting praise not only makes people feel good but it makes them look good in the eyes of others. This generates more trust they have in you, more commitment to you, and more appreciation for you. When you praise someone in front of their friends, teammates, classmates, or peers, you'll see them smile. Your praise uplifts them. Whispering criticism on the other hand may not uplift them, but it's necessary to make them better. Instead of making them feel "less than" by demeaning them in front of their peers, you help them become more by sharing what they need to hear in private. You aren't criticizing to focus on what's wrong but rather to make the wrongs right.

Of course, there will be times that you need to address or coach someone publicly, but you do so not to demean them but to demand the best in them and others. During these moments, you aren't criticizing. You are coaching them and addressing mistakes that everyone can learn from. This makes the person, the team, and you better. When you shout praise and whisper criticism, you elevate others and your own leadership and impact.

60

Don't Let the Good Get in the Way of the Great

There are a lot of things you can do that would be *good*. There are jobs you can choose that you would be *good* at. There are *good* opportunities out there for you. Good is good. Good is average. Good is nice but boring. Good doesn't stir the soul. Good doesn't wake you up in the morning excited to attack the day. Good is fear disguised as smart and safe. Good whispers to you at night that *You are accepting your life instead of creating it.* Good is the regret you feel on your deathbed that you settled. You could have been great but you let the good get in the way of the great.

Ask yourself right now, do you want good or great? Do you want a good life or do you want a great life? Years ago, I owned four restaurants and I remember asking myself whether this was what I truly wanted. If I were to keep going on this path, I'd own 10 to 20 restaurants. I'd make a bunch of money. I'd be successful. But was this what I wanted? I'm good at marketing and operating restaurants, and all I'd have to do was to continue implementing the same formula and I'd create a really good business and a good life. Yet, deep down, I knew this was not what I truly wanted and so my answer was no, I was not going to open more restaurants. I would sell them and pursue becoming a writer and speaker. My wife was scared. "What if it doesn't work?" she asked me.

I explained, "There are no other options." I had to go for this. I didn't want good; I wanted something great. I told myself that even if it took 10 years to be a success, at least I'll be pursuing what I truly wanted and would be striving to be great at something, rather than settling for something I was good at.

If you're reading this, you know I thankfully made the right decision. I'm telling you this story because I want you to make the right decisions, too. Every day you have a choice between good and great. Make it a habit to choose to be great. Make it a habit to pursue the less traveled path to a great life. Ask yourself in every decision, is this what I truly want? Am I settling for good or pursuing great? The more you make this a habit, the more you won't let the good get in the way of the great, and this will lead to your greatest future!

61

Care More

I wrote a book called *The Carpenter* but it's really about being a craftsman. What's the difference? A carpenter builds things. But a craftsman puts their heart and soul, spirit, and passion into their work to create a masterpiece.

The truth is, it's easier to just show up. It's easier to go through the motions at work, at home, in your job, or in your sport. It's easier to be mediocre. But nobody remembers average. Going through the motions won't make an impact. Just showing up doesn't lead to greatness. Michelangelo said, "If people knew how hard I worked to get my mastery, it wouldn't seem so wonderful at all."

It's hard to be great and greatness requires hard work. When speaking to a Major League Baseball team during spring training, I asked, "Who believes they can work harder than they are?" Everyone raised their hand. The manager and coaches were surprised. They were paying these players millions of dollars and here they were saying that they could work harder. So I asked the players, "Why aren't you working harder?" We discussed it and concluded that in order to be motivated to work harder, people have to care more. When you care more you'll give more, do more, and create more.

When Steve Jobs was a boy, his father built a fence in the backyard. Steve noticed that his father was using the finest wood and applying special care for the back of the fence just like the front. Steve asked his dad why he was doing this since no one would see it and no one would know. Steve's dad looked at him and said, "You will know. I will know."

Steve said it was a defining moment in his life and is the reason why he designed Apple products with such craftsmanship and care. Even the inside of the iPhone is designed beautifully because Steve was a craftsman. In fact, Apple's chief designer, Jonathan Ive, famously said, "We believe that our customers can sense the care we have put into our product and design."

When you're a craftsman in a world of carpenters, people will see and know that you care more and clamor for your craftsmanship and what you create, produce, and sell. Apple has sold billions of dollars' worth of products because Steve Jobs cared more. And here's the great news. You can make it a habit to care more, too. See yourself as a craftsman and dedicate yourself to your craft. Have a desire to get better. Show up each day, and put your heart and soul into your work. Care more, do more, and you'll become more. I'm excited to see what you create!

62

Spend Time with Great Friends

Health experts say that loneliness is a new epidemic, and equivalent to smoking 15 cigarettes a day. We have more ways to connect than ever and yet people are feeling more disconnected than ever. We saw the dangers of disconnection during the pandemic of 2020 when so many were isolated, alone and disconnected from others. The truth is that we are not meant to go through life alone. We are made for relationships. We are meant to be connected with others, and when we are not our mental health can suffer.

During the pandemic I flew up to Boston and drove to Cape Cod to see my friends from college who gathered from different parts of the country. We hadn't gotten together in a long time and it was so good to see each other. We played golf, walked on the beach, enjoyed delicious lobster rolls, talked about our kids, and recalled funny stories from our college days. It was a life-changing and soul-nurturing trip. For years I had been charging hard, writing alone, speaking on the road, and traveling from city to city most of the year. I rarely got together with friends, and as a result wasn't living my best life.

I realized during the pandemic how important relationships were and how I needed to make it a habit to get together with friends. In the last 5 years I've gotten together with friends more times than I did in the previous 25 years combined and have felt and seen the difference in my life. Whether it's a trip, a dinner, a wedding, pickleball, a sporting event, or some other gathering, I mark it on my calendar and I make time for it, and it has made me a much happier person.

Don't let life keep you separated. Don't let busyness, stress, and your to-do list keep you from making time with friends that will enhance your happiness, health, and wholeness. Cure loneliness by spending less time alone and more time with people you love and who care about you. The fact is, you can be in a room filled with strangers and still feel lonely, but getting together with one good friend makes you feel alive. So remember, it's not just about getting together with people. It's about *connecting* with people. It's about getting together with friends with whom you share a strong bond.

And this doesn't mean you shouldn't enjoy moments and times of solitude. Perhaps you like being alone. That's a good thing. But you're not meant to go through life feeling alone and lonely. If you find yourself feeling lonely even when you're chatting with friends on social media, know that's it's time to get together with good friends and get a happiness boost. Since loneliness is an epidemic, getting together with good friends is good medicine that will enhance your health.

63

Clear the Clutter

I found myself surrounded by 14 years' worth of boxes, memories, and "Why did we keep this?" moments. After living in the same house for over a decade, my family and I were moving, and truth be told, I *dreaded* it. I spent hours sorting through old belongings, loading things into storage, and debating with my wife (lovingly, of course) about what to keep and what to let go.

I like to get rid of things. My wife likes to keep things. It was exhausting, but it was also enlightening. Because what started as a physical move became a meaningful lesson. We all accumulate things—physically, mentally, emotionally. Stuff that served us in one season but now just takes up space. And the truth is, if we don't make room, we can't move forward. It's essential to make it a habit to clear clutter from our life. To do this, *take inventory of what's taking up space*. Ask yourself:

Is this still serving me?
Do I ever use it and will I ever use it?
Does this mindset, relationship, responsibility, or thing energize me or drain me?
Am I holding on to something just because I always have?
Is this in my way?

Sometimes the greatest breakthroughs come not from adding more, but from letting go. When life is cluttered, we feel stuck. When you free up your space, you free up your mind. When you remove things that are in the way you feel lighter, freer, and more energized to take on the day. Clear the clutter from your workspace, home, car, schedule, mind, and soul and you'll live and lead with greater power.

64

Commit to a Bigger Scoreboard

As I watch sporting events and speak to teams during training camp, I'm reminded that we are wired to have a scoreboard. Humans desire to make and measure progress. I believe there are two scoreboards that we utilize during our life. The first scoreboard is all about winning, success, personal performance, individual accomplishments, and status.

Salespeople love to measure their sales while they hit and surpass their goals. Athletes, coaches, and fans measure wins and losses, performance metrics, touchdowns, points, personal records, and a number of other stats that determine their progress and status. Business leaders measure profit, loss, KPIs, market share, growth, and so on. Doctors measure the number of successful surgeries performed. Teachers, students, schools, and parents measure grades and test scores. And yes, writers like me get excited when our book hits a bestseller list.

We are all utilizing the first scoreboard to measure our progress. The most successful people I know have a competitive spirit. They want to get better. They want to succeed. They want to win! They want to be the best. There was a time when I thought that living according to the first scoreboard was selfish but now I realize it's essential for us to learn how to compete, strive, and fight through adversity so we can eventually thrive according to the second and bigger scoreboard.

As we go through life progressing, measuring, succeeding, fighting, failing, and overcoming, we begin to sense that there is more than just winning and succeeding, and this leads us to the other scoreboard. The second and more significant scoreboard is all about impact and legacy. It's about others, not yourself.

Dabo Swinney, head football coach at Clemson, is the most competitive person I know. He told me that his purpose as a coach is not about winning championships. According to him, it's about "being a great husband and father and using his platform in coaching and education to develop generational leaders." Yes, he wants to win according to the first scoreboard, but the bigger scoreboard that drives him and his program is the legacy and impact he will have on his players.

I was recently at an event speaking with Candace Cameron Bure, a very successful actress and movie and television producer. She mentioned on stage that she's been a gritty fighter her entire life and now she's fighting to make movies and television shows that make an impact. I told her after our talks that everything in her life brought her to this moment, to be someone who would make the kind of positive movies the world needs now.

The first scoreboard teaches us how to compete so we can build the resilience and grit necessary to put up great numbers on our bigger scoreboard. The fight leads us to fighting for others. The desire to compete becomes a mission to help others win. Chasing success leads to leaving a legacy and making an impact. The first scoreboard prepares us for the second scoreboard and bigger wins.

How are you measuring yourself and your life? We need both scoreboards, but ask yourself how you can commit to a bigger scoreboard. Make it habit to commit to the bigger scoreboard daily. Remind yourself what you're fighting for. Remember what a bigger win is all about. Keep score on the bigger scoreboard and let that drive your intentions and actions. When you make it a habit to commit to a bigger scoreboard, you live a much bigger life and make a bigger impact. Most of all, you win where it matters most!

65

Love Tough

I believe in tough love. If you're a leader, manager, coach, teacher, or parent, caring about someone often requires you to challenge and push them to improve, grow, and reach their full potential.

Even the best athletes in the world have a coach to push them. But for tough love to work, love must come first. We must love tough to bring out the best in those we lead!

If people know you care about them, they will be more receptive to you pushing them. On the other hand, if you put tough before love you're more likely to face resistance. As leadership expert Andy Stanley says, "Rules without relationship leads to rebellion." The old dictator-tough style of leadership, without love, no longer works.

Having spent time with a number of professional and college sports teams, I have clearly seen that even athletes who seem to have it all want to know that their coach cares about them. The best coaches love their players and their players know it and play harder and are more loyal to that coach.

The same is true for education and business. Research shows that test scores go up when students have a relationship with their teacher. Numerous engagement surveys show that people are more engaged at work when they know their manager cares about them.

To elevate yourself and those you lead, keep pushing your people to be their best. If you're a parent like me, keep pushing your kids to reach their full potential. Your team needs your toughness to grow! But remember to put love first. Make relationships a priority.

Your love will create the right conditions for growth to happen! Love + Tough = Growth for everyone!

66

Ask Yourself Four Questions Each Day

Everyone wants to get better. Everyone says they want to improve. But those who actually do so are the ones who commit to getting better. They make it a habit to get better. To help make self-improvement a habit, you'll want to ask yourself three questions each day:

1. What did I do well today?

2. What could I do better?

3. What did I learn that will make me better?

After asking and answering those three questions and writing down the answers, you'll want to ask one more question.

- What action will I take tomorrow that will make me better?

The next day, take the action you said will make you better. As you implement this process over time, this habit will lead to actions that contribute to continuous improvement and growth. You won't just talk about getting better. You won't just journal about getting better. You won't just hope to get better. You won't just tell the world what you're going to do to get better. You will actually get better by putting words in action, and your habits and actions will lead to results.

67

Tell Yourself a Positive Story

The story you tell yourself defines the life that you live. Each day you will face obstacles, challenges, and circumstances that can derail you if you let the situation define you and your story. Instead, you must tell yourself a positive story to define and overcome your situation.

We are all living a movie. Your movie can be a drama, a horror story, a documentary, or you can make it an inspirational tale. In the horror story and inspirational tale the hero gets knocked down. But in the inspirational tale the hero gets back up and, armed with optimism and belief, overcomes their challenges and creates a better future for themselves and the world.

To rise above your circumstances and go to the next level, it's essential to see yourself as a hero in your own epic positive story. Your positive story and inspirational tale will include pain, defeat, loss, sadness, rejection, and tragedy, but it will also include you overcoming these situations and challenges with love, purpose, meaning, optimism, resilience, and hope.

By making it a habit to tell yourself a positive story you become the narrator of your life. You don't let adversity put a period where God put a comma. You see the bad and look for the good. You see the conflict and know it's part of your growth as a hero. You see those who will benefit from the lessons you have learned and are learning. You keep writing the positive story you're telling yourself, and as a result your story becomes one worth telling.

68

Be a Giver and a Receiver

In the world of electronics there are resistors and conductors. Resistors' power comes from their electrons but because they hold on to their electrons, resistors have limited power. Conductors freely give and receive electrons, so their power comes from the current that moves through them and thus they have greater power. You can be a resistor and hold on to what you have, or you can be a conductor, give and receive, and experience greater power in your life.

Being a conductor where you become a giver and receiver is a difficult habit for most of us. We don't want to give what we have. We want to hold on to what's ours. We fear giving because we worry that it won't come back to us. We don't want to give and have less. We want to hold on and accumulate more. We want more time, more money, more stuff, more of more. We believe the myth that the key to more is to hold on and not freely give. But when we do this we become a resistor and experience limited power.

The way to have more is to become a conductor and give freely. When you give, you receive and experience more power in your life. I experienced this starting in my 30s when my wife and I began donating 10% of our income to various charities and our church. When we started giving we didn't have much money. It was painful. I was a resistor and always feared not having enough. We always fought about money and our lack of it. But when we decided to start giving money to different causes, something interesting happened. Fear was replaced by trust. We gave and believed that somehow, some way, we would have enough to live on and cover our bills. The next year we received more income than the year before and gave more away. The next year our income grew and we gave even more away. The more we gave, the more we received, allowing us to give away even more year after year. Trusting and giving freely changed our internal nature from resistor to conductor and allowed us to receive and experience this powerful process. What we give today is ten times as much as our total income back when we started.

It's important to realize that even though I'm using money as an example, this isn't even about money. Money is just a form of energy. It's about your mindset, intention, and whether you're fueled by fear or trust. It's about giving your time, energy, and support to others, realizing that what you receive is so much greater. It's about giving to others and trusting there is more than enough for you. Too many go through life holding on to what they have and thus don't receive what others have for them. We think if we give our time, energy, and support, that's taking away from our success, but in reality it's expanding and growing it. It's not why you do it. It's just how things work. You don't give to receive. But when you give generously of your time, money, support, and energy, you receive generously and you have more to give.

Now, I know what some of you might be thinking. "I give and it doesn't come back to me, or the person I give to takes me for granted and doesn't appreciate it. They use me and take advantage of me." First and foremost, the key is to give generously but not recklessly. You can be generous and prudent at the same time. Then, when you give to the right people and causes, you want to give without expectation. You don't give to get. When you do this you're still a resistor. Instead, just give to give without holding on to any expectation. Some won't appreciate it. Others will not recognize what you did for them. They won't appreciate how you gave your time, money, and energy to support them. You may not receive from them, but as you give without expectation, watch how it comes back to you in other ways from other sources. When you give generously you'll receive generously. It's how things work!

And I also want to encourage you to make it a habit to receive as well. Some feel bad about receiving. They like to give but feel guilty about receiving. They think it's selfish to receive. Or they don't feel like they deserve it. But not receiving is just as selfish as not giving. When you don't receive, you cut off the flow of energy that is meant to flow through you to others. Just as you must give generously, you must receive willingly. Make it a habit to give and receive. Be a conductor and watch the power move through you and your life!

69

Make the Pie Bigger

Too many people focus on getting their piece of the pie, but a key to growing exponentially is to focus on making the pie bigger. You don't fight for your piece. You create a bigger pie so there is more for you and for everyone. This requires an abundant mindset and the belief that this is a big universe with boundless ever-expanding pies available to you. There are ideas, resources, opportunities, businesses, and energy that are available to you and waiting to be tapped. With so much available to us, why do we expect so little? Let's not think small. Let's think big and create a bigger opportunity.

When I was speaking to the Clemson football team, Dabo Swinney, the head coach, told me about this guy Damon West who had just spoken to his team about the carrot, the egg, and the coffee bean. As he told me this story I got a vision for a book called *The Coffee Bean*. I saw the cover and it had my name and Damon West's name on it. I didn't know Damon but I got his number from Dabo and called him. I said we should do a book together called *The Coffee Bean*. Damon said, "That's nice of you, Jon, but you don't need to do this book with me. I'm a nobody and everyone I know has read your books. You can do it yourself." I said, "Damon, I know we are supposed to do this book together and I want to give you 50% of the advance and royalties." Damon kept wondering what the catch was, but there was no catch. I knew we were supposed to do the book together and I wasn't going to take the whole pie.

Damon had spent seven years in prison before this happened and he has an incredible story that he shares in his talks. His parents had done everything they could, including spending a lot of their savings to try to keep him out of prison, but Damon willingly and humbly had to serve his time for the crimes he committed. He's not proud of what he did but he's become a better man for it. When Damon received 50% of the advance from our publisher for *The Coffee Bean*, he gave it to his parents. Amazingly, it was the same amount that his parents had spent on his legal fees to try to keep him out of prison.

Since that time, Damon has been speaking all around the country and the world on *The Coffee Bean* and the book has become a mega-bestseller. My 50% share of *The Coffee Bean* is greater than the 100% share of some of my other books. By partnering with Damon I made the pie bigger. By giving, I gained. By making the pie bigger Damon is living his purpose, and together we are making a greater impact.

I want to encourage you to make it a habit to make the pie bigger in all that you do. Look for ways to create win-win relationships and opportunities where everyone can win and everyone can grow. In negotiations, share ideas to make the pie bigger. Consistently look for new ways, new opportunities, and new ideas that will expand the pie you have. The bigger the pie, the more you can share. And when hiring, look for people who will help you make the pie bigger and be incentivized when it grows! This leads to a bigger pie and a bigger piece for everyone.

70

Focus on Winning People Instead of Arguments

What good is it to win an argument if you lose the person in the process? Your ego may feel better but your life gets worse. Relationships are everything, and if you would rather win an argument and lose the relationship, eventually you won't have friends to argue with. People don't want to spend time with those who care more about winning than about them. They want to be around and invest their time in those who listen to them, respect them, and care about them even if they disagree with them. The person who is always right is often alone.

I have a few friends who love to argue. They love to be right. I made a decision not to argue or debate them. It felt like a waste of energy every time we argued. And I don't need to be right. I would rather have fun with my friends than argue with them. The funny thing is, they often call me and want to hang out and I don't go out of my way to spend time with them. I don't want to win the argument. I want to win the person.

In a world where there's more fighting than ever over politics, religion, and various topics, make it a habit to focus on winning the person instead of the argument. Find out what's truly important to them. Ask them why they think the way they do. Understand where their thought process is coming from. You may disagree with them, but you can empathize with them. The argument is often not even about the argument. There is usually much more underneath the surface that is causing the argument in the first place. When you ask questions, listen, and care, you won't win the argument, but you will win the person and prevent arguments from happening. Most of all, when you love people more than you love being right, you are the one who wins in the end!

71

Take a Power Nap

In a culture that celebrates grinding, hustling, and pushing through, naps get a bad reputation. They're seen as lazy, indulgent, or unnecessary. But the truth is that they are strategic if used right! It's not always about doing more; it's about recovering better to have more energy, stamina, and focus for the daily climb.

Done right, a nap is an incredible tool for productivity and presence. But here's the key: Naps only work if they honor the body's most important rhythm. Justin Roethlingshoefer, a leading proactive health expert and author of *Holy Health*, explains it clearly: "Naps are amazing, but only if they don't disrupt the most important rhythm we have, the circadian rhythm. This is the governing rhythm that the entire body works off of." When naps ignore that rhythm, they steal from the night. When naps align with it, they give you back your life and your energy.

Timing Is Everything

When it comes to naps, timing is everything. Not all naps are created equal. Justin says there are only two effective nap lengths: around 20 minutes and around 90 minutes. Nothing in between. Why? Because the body operates in sleep cycles that last about 90 minutes. A short nap (around 20 minutes) refreshes the brain without pulling you into deep sleep. A longer nap (around 90 minutes) allows you to complete a full cycle, including REM, so you wake up restored instead of groggy.

The danger zone is 30–60 minutes. That's where you fall into deep sleep but don't finish the cycle. That's when you wake up foggy, sluggish, and worse than before. A great nap should leave you clearer, calmer, and more focused—not disoriented.

When to Nap

When to nap is also crucial to make napping work for you. This rule is the game changer, especially for parents, leaders, and anyone running on limited sleep. To find your ideal nap window, do this:

- Identify the time you typically fall asleep.
- Identify the time you typically wake up.
- Find the midpoint between those two times.
- Add 12 hours.

For example:

- If you usually sleep from 10 p.m. to 6 a.m., your midpoint is 2 a.m.
- Because the circadian rhythm operates on a roughly 12-hour clock, your optimal nap window is 12 hours later—around 2 p.m.

- This timing works *with* your biology, not against it. It gives you restoration without stealing from your nighttime sleep.

A good nap doesn't just restore energy. It restores patience. It restores presence and power. It restores decision-making. Here are a few tips to make the habit of taking a power nap even more beneficial:

- Nap in darkness or with an eye mask: Light tells your brain to stay alert. Darkness accelerates recovery.

- Keep legs slightly elevated: This helps circulation and speeds nervous system recovery.

- No guilt allowed: Guilt activates stress. Stress cancels the benefit. Rest is an unselfish act because it allows you to give more to the world.

72

Be Still and Be Silent

Rubin "Hurricane" Carter said, "When you're in solitary confinement and you're six feet under without light, sound, or running water, there is no place to go but inside. And when you go inside, you discover that everything that exists in the universe is also within you." Rubin was wrongfully imprisoned and tragically spent 18 years in prison, yet while there he discovered the power that comes from being still and sitting in silence.

When was the last time you sat in silence and heard the sound of your breath and felt the stillness of your soul? If you're like most people, it's probably been a while. The fact is we live in a busy, noisy world filled with the sounds of sirens, TVs, ringtones, and notifications. We know we need to slow down for our health and happiness, yet it often seems impossible. We've become so addicted to busyness, noise, "doing," and "achieving" that we've forgotten how to just "be" and "rest." We've forgotten how good it truly feels to be still and silent. No to-do list. No past. No future. Just resting and recharging *now*.

Let's make this a daily habit. Five to 10 minutes will give you hours of benefits and priceless productivity. Each day, decide to jump off the treadmill of life, shut off the phone, turn off the computer, pause the rat race, and find a brief moment of silence and experience the power that comes with it. At first you may feel like jumping out of your skin. If this is the case, know that means you need to do this more than anyone. Each moment that we fill with noise, instead of silence, is a lost opportunity for enhanced energy, focus, and mental clarity. For within silence sits the energy to recharge our batteries—to refuel our tired lives, to help us renew and create. Best of all, stillness and silence are cheaper than a double latte, more energizing than an energy drink, and more available than any fuel supply on the planet. Silence and stillness are always waiting for you. They are a moment and decision away. Decide to be still, be silent, be renewed!

73

Do a Daily Dead Hang

Who would have thought that hanging from a pole could be so beneficial? But that's what the research tells us. A stronger grip strength means a longer, healthier life, usually because it requires a lifestyle involving lifting, carrying, and moving. In a world that rewards tension, gripping things we can't control, and carrying the weight of responsibility, most people never fully let go. Their shoulders stay elevated. Their breath stays shallow. Their nervous system stays on edge.

The two-minute dead hang is the opposite. It's not flashy. It's not exhausting. But it's a simple, powerful habit that produces great health results. Leading proactive health expert Justin Roethlingshoefer told me that I must put this habit in the book because the dead hang gives your body the muscle it needs to thrive, now and as you age. And this includes both physical and neurological muscles. Modern life compresses the body. Sitting, driving, using devices, stress, and poor posture all load the spine and shoulders. The dead hang reverses that. Research shows that hanging:

- Decompresses the spine, reducing disk pressure and back pain
- Improves shoulder mobility and joint integrity

- Stimulates grip strength, a powerful predictor of longevity and all-cause mortality
- Activates the parasympathetic nervous system when paired with slow breathing

To do a dead hang, Jusin recommends that we:

- Find a pull-up bar, rings, or anything sturdy overhead.
- Grip with hands shoulder-width apart.
- Let your body fully relax. No shrugging, no pulling.
- Breathe slowly through your nose.
- Accumulate two **total** minutes per day.
  - Beginners: Break it into 10- to 30-second rounds. **Important: Make sure you talk to your medical practitioner before doing this exercise, and avoid doing it if you are pregnant or have elbow, wrist, or shoulder issues.**
  - Advanced: Aim for one continuous 2-minute hang.

Grip strength alone has been repeatedly linked to longer life span, better cardiovascular health, and lower risk of injury as we age. And unlike complicated programs, the dead hang costs nothing and takes two minutes. It teaches your body how to let go both physically and emotionally. No forcing. No pain. The goal is decompression, health, and becoming stronger for longer. Do it alone or invite a friend or family member to "hang out" with you sometime and share the benefits with them.

DO A DAILY DEAD HANG

74

Be a Lifelong Teacher

Everyone says to be a lifelong student. I agree with this and believe it's essential to always be learning and growing. But I also believe you will learn and grow the most when you become a lifelong teacher. Experts will tell you that you learn the most when you have to teach a subject to others. To teach it you have to learn it, know it, understand the nuances associated with your topic, have answers to questions, and be able to defend your position. The more you teach a topic, the more you realize what you don't know and need to know, which leads you to learning more and knowing more.

I have a master's in teaching and taught in a middle school for a year. After that I opened up a bar and restaurant and became an entrepreneur. But to this day I still consider myself a teacher. My subjects just happen to be culture, mindset, leadership, teamwork, and positive habits! The more I've taught others, the more I have grown in exponential ways. The more I learn, the more I know, the more I teach, the more I grow.

I've also seen this with many of the certified trainers who've joined my team. They started out as students, became teachers, and now are elevating their life, career, and impact in amazing ways. The person they are when they start pales in comparison to who they become in just a year of training and teaching others. You can see their confidence increase, their stature among their peers rise, and their income and impact grow significantly. I also saw it with my own daughter, who started doing speaking engagements and teaching my programs at 25. She gained massive confidence and exponentially grew in a short amount of time by teaching others. Now she's helping leaders and organizations with their culture, mindset, leadership, and teamwork.

Ironically, the greatest self-growth strategy of all is to help others grow. To become a lifelong teacher, pick a subject you want to teach. What do you love to learn and share with others? Identify whom you want to help. Become a mentor to others in your organization. Start a coaching group. Create a mastermind group. Become an expert in a topic that is essential for your company or organization and start teaching others about it. Become a lifelong mentor, teacher, or coach and commit yourself to helping others grow and you will grow the most.

75

Reduce or Stop Drinking

I didn't want to write this. I don't like telling people what not to do. I'd rather share positive habits that would be beneficial, not talk about a habit that can be harmful. But if I didn't mention this, I'd be doing you a disservice. Perhaps you need to hear this or someone you know needs to hear this, and perhaps me writing this will be the catalyst that gets you to reduce or stop drinking, leading to you improving and growing in incredible ways. Knowing this is a strong possibility, and writing this with care and not judgment, I'm willing to share a hard truth that may not be popular. And the truth is that alcohol too often limits your health and potential. Sure, there are some like my friend from college who can drink all night and then run a marathon the next day. But for most of us, alcohol makes us more tired, more depressed, and more cluttered, and less motivated, less driven, and less healthy. Health experts label alcohol a neurotoxin and carcinogen that damages organs like the liver, brain, and digestive tract, even with moderate use.

I remember meeting a college football coach in South Florida for the first time. He asked me for advice on how to get back to the next level because he had been there before and was on the rise again. I said that he needed to stop drinking. I explained how it was holding him back and affecting various areas of his life. I told him I'd understand if he didn't want to hear this and that I'd leave right away. He paused and said, "Stay, I need to hear it." We had a great talk and have been great friends ever since.

He didn't act on this advice right away but eventually gave up drinking, and as I write this he is now at the top of the college football world. Six months after he stopped drinking, he told me how everything in his life became easier. He said, "I have so much more clarity and reality just looks and feels different. Life was blurry but now it's like high definition." I watched as he became a better coach, a better father, and a better leader. One anti-habit of not drinking led to many healthy habits that elevated him and his life.

I have zero judgment for those who drink and I will have a glass of wine or a tequila, lime juice, and soda myself a few times a year. I write this only to say that if you want to elevate every area of your life and grow exponentially, you likely will want to reduce or stop drinking. You know yourself the best, so ask yourself, "Is alcohol keeping me from being the best I can be?" If so, then the answer is simple. Reduce it or stop it. See how you feel. See what you accomplish. If it works for you, keep doing it. I've never had anyone say they regretted giving up or limiting alcohol. I've only heard people tell me they accomplished more and felt better than ever. So think about it, try it, and see if it works for you.

Because alcohol is so pervasive and such a huge part of our society and culture, it's difficult not to drink when you're at a dinner, cocktail reception, party, or other social situation. My go-to drink is sparkling water in a wine glass with a lime. I wake up with no regrets and feeling great and ready to take on the day.

76

Value Everyone

If you believe that everyone has value, then you will value everyone. Not just the CEO, billionaire, online influencer, athlete, or celebrity, but also the janitor, cashier, waitress, bus driver, landscaper, and receptionist. When you value everyone, you see the worth inside each person. Beyond the status, title, influence, followers, money, and power, you see the priceless person. You acknowledge them. You appreciate them. You get to know their name. I've found that the more we see the value in everyone and add value to them, the more life brings back amazing value to us. It's the law of reciprocity. Value others. Add value and value comes back to you. It's not why you do it, but it's how it works.

I had just spoken to the Los Angeles Dodgers during spring training and needed to get to the airport. My Uber pulled up the second I walked outside and I hopped into the car. It was a nice car and I asked my driver what made her decide to become an Uber driver. I know everyone has a story and I valued hers. It turned out Marlo's husband had lost his job and she was driving to support her family while he found another job. I asked her a few more questions, liked her responses, and offered her a part-time job to help me out with my podcast and help my assistant. She accepted and it allowed her to be at home with her kids. My assistant was a little surprised when I told her that I had hired my Uber driver to help with my podcast, but after a few months she saw that Marlo was resourceful and helpful. A year later my assistant had to step down to care for her dad. At the time I didn't know if Marlo could handle all that the job required but she's done a tremendous job ever since and has become one of my most trusted and valuable team members! I valued her and now she brings value to my team, my company, and my clients every day.

Recently, at a dinner event, I saw the power of valuing everyone. I was seated at a long table across from a guy who wasn't talking to anyone. He seemed shy and honestly I felt bad for him. I was looking forward to a great dinner and conversation and was wondering why I picked this seat. But then I reminded myself to value everyone and engage him and help him enjoy his dinner rather than worrying about mine. I smiled at him and said hello and asked him his name. Brian, he told me. I said it was great to meet him and asked a few questions. We talked, and in the middle of a great conversation the host came to say hello to Brian and talked about Brian performing at a future event. It turns out shy Brian was actually Grammy-winning musician and songwriter Brian McKnight. I laughed at myself and the situation. Here I felt bad for Brian, who wasn't talking to anyone, when millions would love to talk to him. Brian certainly didn't need me to talk to him to feel better about his life. He was doing just fine. But because I valued him as a person, regardless of who he was, I now have a valuable and wonderful friendship with him.

Make it a habit to value everyone and you'll see how it comes back to you in amazing ways. It doesn't always happen immediately, but over time you'll see every aspect of your life become more valuable.

77

Elevate Your Circle

We often hear that you must surround yourself with the right people if you want to grow, and it's true that the people you surround yourself with will either help you soar or lead to your crash. So, yes, if you want to grow yourself exponentially, you want to make sure you elevate your circle. The right circle will determine how high and how fast you rise. But for this to happen in the beginning, it's less about people surrounding you and more about you surrounding the people you want to be around. Those people aren't going out of their way to look for you. You must look for and find them. You look for the people you want to learn from and be around and find groups they are a part of and join those groups if possible. And what you find is that when you get in the same room and same groups as those people, you'll be exposed to new ideas, new ways of thinking, new friendships, new opportunities, and new levels of growth available to you. When you elevate your circle, you'll elevate your life.

I had never been a part of a mastermind group before, but shortly after the pandemic I began getting invited to speak to various mastermind groups and coaching communities. While I was there, I would sit and listen to other speakers and meet various people who were part of the groups. I loved it, and I loved seeing them learn, grow, and connect with each other. I began to ask myself what I would do differently if I started my own group. And that's how my circle was born. Since that time I've watched wonderful people meet, connect, and grow incredible friendships. With groups like this you're one person, one idea, one relationship away from improving your life, and what I love most is seeing people grow with each other. In fact, I did a teaching session with my circle on habits that will exponentially grow them, and that teaching led to me writing this book.

You don't have to join my circle to grow, but I do encourage you to find or create a circle that will help you elevate yourself and others. In addition to my own circle, I get together with different groups of college and pro coaches, entrepreneurs, authors, and business leaders. For the first 50 years of my life I never did this. In the last 5 years I've done it often and have grown more in 5 years than the previous 50. That's the power of a circle. That's the power of elevating whom you learn from and grow with. That's the power of making this a habit.

78

Learn from Everyone

After I moved to Jacksonville, Florida, with my family and opened a few restaurants, my friend's father kept encouraging me to meet his friend Harris Rosen, who owned hotels in Orlando. So one day I drove to Orlando to meet Harris Rosen in his office. As I sat across from him, he looked at me curiously and asked flippantly, "And you're here because?"

After an awkward pause that felt like an eternity, I said, "Mr. Berkery encouraged me to come meet you and I like to learn from successful people, so here I am. I just opened up a few Moe's Southwest Grill franchises in Jacksonville and it's going pretty well."

He then began to ask me questions about how I was running and marketing the business. I told him how I was collecting emails from my guests and adding them to an email newsletter and when I opened a new location I would email everyone a free burrito coupon that they could email and share with others. Whenever we opened a new location we would have a line of people with their emailed coupons. It was instant marketing and instant customers!

Harris picked up his phone, called one of his employees, and told him what I said. Then he asked, "Are we doing this?" When he heard that the answer was no, he chuckled as he looked at me, shook his head, and said, "You never know. You never know." In essence he was saying he was really surprised that this meeting turned out to be beneficial for him, and you never know where your next idea will come from and whom it will come from.

It's a lesson I never forgot and have put into practice. I believe in learning from everyone and seeing everyone as a teacher who can teach you something if you're willing to take the time to ask questions and learn. When you make this a habit, you receive all sorts of ideas from unlikely sources, and you never stop learning and growing!

79

Ask for and Receive Feedback

Blind spots don't only exist when you're driving a car. They also happen when you can't see improvements you need to make. It's hard to evaluate yourself and to identify all the ways you need to improve. Even the most self-aware person will have blind spots in their leadership, relationships, parenting, communication, job performance, and interactions. That's why feedback from others is essential.

As my mentor Ken Blanchard said, "Feeback is the breakfast of champions." You need it to be great. Don't fear feedback because it might be critical. Welcome it knowing it makes you better. Don't see it as defining you but rather as a tool for refining you. Regularly ask your team, customers, colleagues, and others for feedback as a way to continuously improve and strive for excellence. Some feedback might be incorrect or the result of someone's warped perspective, so you don't always want to make decisions based on one person's feedback, but I've found that if you continually ask for feedback, you'll see a pattern emerge of what is working well and what you need to do to improve. The path to growth will be clear.

Notice that this habit includes two parts. First, you must ask for feedback. Most won't give you feedback unless you ask for it. I like to say, "Help me get better," or "How can we better help you?" or "Please read this and let me know what it's missing," or "What should I do differently in my talk?" The feedback over the years has been invaluable.

The second part is receiving feedback. When it's given, make sure you receive it. Don't deflect it. Don't argue about it. Don't let it bounce off you. Receive it and reflect on it. Is it from a trusted reliable source? Does it have merit? Is it valid? Think of what you can do differently and whether this would make you better. Write it down. Embrace it. Take action on it. Consuming your feedback like this allows it to nourish you so you can become a champion!

80

Eliminate the Waste

Every healthy system includes the removal of waste. Whether that's from our bodies, the weekly trash removal from our homes and neighborhoods, or a company that closes its lowest-performing stores every year, the removal of waste is essential for health and thriving. Just as we have to remove the clutter in our life, we must also remove the waste. Waste is clutter that becomes harmful and toxic if you hold on to it too long. Waste is the bad relationship that is destroying your confidence and holding you back. Waste is the friend that really isn't a friend and wants to see you fail. Waste is the bad habit that keeps you from positive habits. Waste is the negative thought pattern keeping you from your dreams. Waste is the past experience keeping you from moving forward and creating an amazing future.

I don't know what your waste is, but I know we all have it and you need to remove it from your life to exponentially grow you! Just as companies conduct waste and efficiency audits, I want to encourage you to do a waste audit of your life. What things are you holding on to that are adding toxic weight? This toxic weight not only makes you feel heavier but it also makes you feel less healthy, less energized, less like yourself. Perhaps you've been carrying around this toxic weight for so long that you've forgotten what normal feels like. It might be hard to let go of what now feels like normal but isn't a good normal. In this case, recruit a few of your best and most trusted friends and family members to help you with the waste audit and identify what needs to go. Then, once you know what needs to go, let the waste go! Don't hold on to it.

Many years ago, on my first book tour, I drove thousands of miles and visited 28 cities. At one point on the journey, I looked in the rearview mirror and realized I had all this stuff on my bus that I didn't need. Why did I travel with all these bags of useless stuff for so long, I wondered? I didn't want to drive heavy. I wanted to travel light. As I drove past Phoenix through the desert I pulled over and found a big trash can and put the bags where they belonged. It felt good to let the bags off the bus. I then got back on the bus with the past behind me and a road full of daylight ahead. A big smile came upon my face. I was now lighter and freer for my future. Letting go let me go faster and farther. I hope you'll do the same!

81

Think Intentionally

The past few years I've spent a lot of time with leadership expert John C. Maxwell, including events we've done together and an annual "football feast" where we travel to three college football games in two days right after Thanksgiving. On our most recent trip I told John I had discovered his superpower. It's the way he thinks. He is very intentional with his thinking. He will carve out time during his day to think about a topic and all the nuances associated with it. He will take an idea I share and think about, add to it, and come back to me with new ways to approach it. We even spent 20 minutes recently talking about the word *devotion*—what it is and isn't and how to define it. When we were finished he said he wanted to think about it some more.

As our football feast group gathered to eat breakfast, John said he was thinking about how at 78 years old he can maximize the next five years of his life and make the biggest impact. He asked us for suggestions so he could think about it. On the plane to one of the games, he shared how he intentionally approaches giving advice to his grandkids, how he decides how much money to give to nonprofits during his lifetime, how he connects with an audience, how he cultivates relationships, and how he thinks about thinking.

I realized that everyone thinks but not everyone thinks intentionally. In fact, very few of us think intentionally, including me. Watching John demonstrate the power of intentional thinking inspired me to be more intentional with my thinking, and I want to help you do the same. After all, if our thoughts create our reality and determine what we create and become, then we should be intentional about what we are thinking about to create the life we want. Thinking intentionally means you think about what matters most. How do you want to approach certain situations? What type of team do you want to build? How will you handle certain situations? What do you want your future to look like? How will you parent your kids? What principles will guide you? Where should you invest your time and energy? What words should you say? Where should you go on vacation? How and where should you invest your money? What friends should you hang out with? The things you can think about intentionally are endless.

The key is to make time for intentional thinking in order to create your life, rather than simply wander through it. This doesn't mean you try to control every aspect of your life. It means you intentionally think about it, decide what's best, and control what you can control. Intentional thinking is a superpower available to all of us. We just have to make time to do it. When you think intentionally, you can design wisely, act decisively, and create powerfully.

82

Add Play to Your Day

My friend and college lacrosse teammate Teddy Berkery tries to answer his phone faster than anyone in his office. It's a game he plays to make work more engaging and fun. Sheldon likes to walk around the gym and tell jokes to all of us on the bikes and treadmills. People who are serious about their workout find themselves laughing. When my kids were growing up I would return home from a speaking engagement and often find my wife and kids dancing around the house to loud music. Homework breaks turned into raves! And these days I love to play pickleball whenever I'm not traveling on the road speaking. I love playing and feel young when I'm battling on the court.

We were born to play. As kids, play was a natural part of the day. No one taught us how to play. We just did it. But as we get older, too many of us forget how to play. The world teaches us not to play and tells us to be serious. Be an adult. There's no time for play! So we stop playing and having fun, and life and work become a chore.

Yes, life is serious. Business is serious. Winning is serious. The work we are here to do is serious. But it can also be fun! And when it's fun you're able to take on the day with less stress, more levity, and a greater perspective. When you add play to your day, you'll experience less burnout, greater productivity, and more energy. There are many ways to add play to your day. Just make it a habit and don't feel guilty. You're not playing and losing focus. You're playing and gaining more clarity. You know the mission. You're serious about it. But you're going to have fun while going after it and as a result you'll be more likely to achieve it.

83

Seize the Moment

I can recall many moments in my life where the pressure of the spotlight was on me and I rose to the occasion and won the game in overtime. I can also remember many moments when I failed under pressure and walked away knowing I didn't do my best.

Oh, how I wish I could go back in time and change my moments of defeat. I wish I was granted a "do-over" and given the opportunity to change history. But that only works in movies. Unfortunately, we can't change the past, but we can create a better future.

In studying the best of the best, I've discovered how and why they have a knack for rising to the occasion when the pressure is the greatest. *They are able to seize the moment.* Whether it's an athletic performance, a presentation to a client, a surgery, a lecture, or a job interview, the best are able to define the moment rather than letting the moment define them. How do they do this?

The best seize the moment because they don't allow their fear of failure to define them. When the best are in the midst of their performance, they are not thinking, "What if I win?" or "What if I lose?" They are not thinking, "What if I make a mistake or fail?" The best are focused solely on the moment. They are one with the moment.

To habitually seize the moment in your life, don't let your failure define you; let it fuel you. Let it push you into the moment and beyond yourself. Let it inspire you to live and work each day as though it was your last. Don't focus on the past, and don't look to the future. Focus on the now. Success, rewards, accolades, fame, and fortune are merely byproducts for those who are able to seize the moment, not those who look beyond it. Ironically, to enjoy success you must not focus on it. Rather, you must focus on the process that produces success. The moment is really all you have, and when you engage and become one with it, you can soar to new heights. When the spotlight is on you, don't worry, don't fear, and don't think. Just do what you do, seize the moment, and the outcome will take care of itself.

84

Create Purpose-Driven Goals

For years I chose Organic Valley milk over other brands in the supermarket. I had no idea why until I spoke at their remote headquarters surrounded by acres of farmland in the middle of Wisconsin. I discovered a company that didn't believe in sales and revenue goals. Of course, they forecasted sales for budgetary, planning, and growth purposes and measured numbers and outcomes, but they did so with the belief that numbers were just a byproduct of how well they were living and sharing their purpose. Instead of focusing on goals with numbers, Organic Valley passionately focused on their purpose-driven goals: providing opportunities for farmers to make a living, sustainability of the land, and providing families with healthy dairy products that were free of hormones and antibiotics. The result: Organic Valley's numbers kept growing and growing.

While speaking to an NFL team, I had each player write their goals on a piece of paper. After a few minutes I had them rip up the paper they had just written on. You could hear the complaints and feel their anger and frustration while they ripped up the paper they had just spent time and energy producing. I then asked, "How many of you wrote down win a Super Bowl, win x number of games, achieve x number of yards, have x number of interceptions, and so on?" All the hands went up. I told them that every person in every NFL meeting room has the same goals. So it's not the goals that will make you successful. Otherwise everyone and every team would be successful after writing down their goals. Instead, it's your commitment to the process, your growth, and your purpose that drives you to reach these goals that will determine what you accomplish.

I then had them write down their commitments and purpose for playing and had them share with the rest of the team. It was powerful.

The truth is that numbers and goals don't drive people. People with a purpose drive the numbers and achieve goals. Research clearly shows that true motivation is driven by meaning and purpose rather than extrinsic rewards, numbers, and goals. A study of West Point alums showed that those who had intrinsic goals ("I want to serve my country and make a difference") outperformed those with extrinsic goals ("I want to rise in the ranks and become an officer because it's prestigious").

Goals may motivate you in the short term but they will not sustain you over time. Without a good reason to keep moving forward during challenges, you either quit or go through the motions like one of the walking dead. This doesn't mean you shouldn't measure numbers or have goals. It's okay to have a goal you want to achieve, but once you identify a goal or outcome, you'll be more powerful and more energized if you focus on your purpose. Your greater purpose will lead to greater performance. Purpose-driven goals sell more milk, win more football games, enhance performance, and lead to outcomes that far surpass your numbered goals.

85

Tell Me Something Good

In our Positive Leadership workshops we do an exercise where we ask participants to "Tell me something good." It's a practice you can also use to turn around a constant complainer, energy vampire, or negative employee, friend, or relative. You know whom I'm talking about: the person who always finds something wrong and wants to tell you about it the second you say hello. While it's important to connect with others, I'm well aware that it's common practice to avoid the person who's always griping.

So what do you do? You don't avoid them. Instead, every time you see them you say, "Tell me something good." They have no choice but to tell you something positive, and the more you ask this, the more they will expect it from you. The next step is to ask them, "What's not good?" This gives them the opportunity to share something that isn't right or something that needs attention, a resolution, or a solution. Asking this question also lets people know that you're not a fake positive leader who ignores reality but rather someone who wants to make their reality better. This leads to the third and final question. "How can we make it good?" Or "What will you do to make it good?" This ensures that the previous question doesn't lead to venting or complaining without identifying possible solutions and actions that will empower them.

There's a lot of negativity and a lot of negative people in the world. Many love to complain and bring others down with them. But by starting conversations with "Tell me something good," you can ward off the negativity and help elevate the people you interact with and the conversations you have!

86

Slay Energy Vampires

If you want to go to the next level, you must make it a habit to defeat energy vampires along the way. Energy vampires are the people who will suck the energy out of you and your vision and mission if you let them. They don't do it with fangs but with negative energy, narcissism, pessimism, discouragement, distraction, and division. Since writing about energy vampires in *The Energy Bus* I've received countless questions on how to slay them, not with weapons or garlic, but with strategies to eliminate and remove them. In this spirit I want to share what has worked, because I've seen too many people's growth and success derailed because of energy vampires, and I don't want that to happen to you.

First and foremost, love them. No one really wants to be an energy vampire. They are likely negative for a reason. The first step should always be to love, understand, and transform. For example, Martin, an executive at a consumer products company, told me that he put a sign on his door that said *Energy Vampires Welcome. Expect to be transformed.*

While I love Martin's approach, I also know that not every energy vampire is willing to change. If your efforts to transform an energy vampire are not successful and they are sabotaging the team and organization, then they should be let off the bus. This doesn't mean you don't care about them. It means you care about everyone the energy vampire is affecting. Over the years I've had countless people let energy vampires off the bus and the team immediately felt lighter and better. One person can't make a team but one person can break a team.

If you don't like the thought of letting people off the bus, you're not alone. That's why I always tell leaders and managers that you won't have to let an energy vampire off the bus if you create a positive culture where energy vampires are uncomfortable being negative. If you create a strong, positive culture that attracts positive people, fosters positive communication, and generates positive energy, the energy vampires who are unwilling to change will walk off the bus themselves because they don't fit in. Energy vampires don't like the light.

An example comes from a school principal who leads one of our Energy Bus Certified schools. She had a very negative teacher who told her, "I've been here before you and I'll be here after you. I'm not changing." The principal asked us for advice and we recommended that she really focus on building a strong positive culture. Get as many teachers to buy in as possible. Get them on the bus. At the end of the year the principal told us that the energy vampire came to her office and resigned. She told the principal, "I can't do this anymore. This place is too positive for me.

I feel like I'm getting run over by the bus." She left and is now on another bus making that school miserable, while the school she left is doing better than ever. Morale has skyrocketed.

The best way to deal with energy vampires in your organization is at the culture level, where you set the expectation that people who drain the energy of others will not be tolerated. One college football coach did this with his football team a few years ago. He had all his players read *The Energy Bus* and he had an artist draw a huge picture of an energy vampire on the wall of their team meeting room. Any time a player was being an energy vampire, they put the player's picture on the wall. No one wanted to be on the wall. In essence, the coach was telling his team that we will not allow negativity to sabotage our team and goals. Leaders must make it clear that negativity that drains others and sabotages team performance is not acceptable. Leaders/managers/coaches/principals must create a positive work environment where their people can do their best work without being affected by an energy vampire.

If you're not a leader or manager and you're not in a position to define the culture or hire and fire people, you're likely wondering what you should do if you have an energy vampire on your team or in your office. In this case you can influence your team and office culture by being more positive than the negativity you face. Share positive energy daily and it will spread to others and eventually the positive energy will surround the energy vampire and they will change or leave.

If one of your friends or a trusted colleague at work is an energy vampire, you may decide to talk to them about their negativity. If you have a strong relationship with them and they know you care about them, they may be open to your advice. But remember that energy vampires can't see their own reflection. They may not realize they are an energy vampire. Proceed with caution if you decide to go this route. And if you do, do it with love. Highlight their positive characteristics first. For a manager we coached, we told her to write a positive letter to her energy vampire and then meet with her. They discussed the positive letter first, which included her strengths and positive attributes, and then the manager shared how her negative energy was affecting the team. It turned out the energy vampire felt isolated and alone on the team and was dealing with personal issues at home. After the conversation, the relationship and the energy vampire were both transformed, and the manager made it a point to connect more with her team one on one.

Finally, but most importantly, if you encounter energy vampires in your daily life, remember Gandhi's words: "I will not let anyone walk through my mind with their dirty feet." No one has the power to make you feel a certain way. The power inside of you is greater than anything outside of you. When you remember this and your positive energy is greater than their negativity, you'll win every battle with an energy vampire and keep rising higher.

87

Serve with a Caring Trademark

Years ago I was taking a walk with my mom near her home in South Florida when I noticed she was getting tired. My mom and I always walked together. She was a fit, walking machine and never got tired, so I knew something was wrong.

"Let's go back to the condo so you can rest," I said.

"No, I want to walk to the store so I can get some food to make you a sandwich for your drive home."

I was headed back to my home in Ponte Vedra Beach and my mom thought I might starve to death without eating during the five-hour drive.

"Okay," I said, knowing she had her mind set. Growing up in a Jewish-Italian family, the one thing you didn't do is argue with Mom about food. To her, food was love.

We continued walking and made it to the supermarket, and as we walked back I could tell she was getting more and more tired. When we arrived back at her condo she was exhausted, and yet the first thing she did was walk into the kitchen to make me a sandwich.

On my drive home I ate her sandwich but didn't think much about it at the time. Now, years later, I think about that sandwich a lot because it was the last time I had a conversation with her. My mom was battling cancer, which was why she was so tired. She didn't tell me how bad it really was, nor did she mention how bleak the odds were for her survival. She was fighting for her life and yet on that day her biggest priority was to make me a sandwich. Looking back, I realize she wasn't just making me a sandwich. She was showing me what selfless love and servant leadership are all about.

At her funeral, many of her real estate clients and colleagues shared countless stories with me of all the selfless acts of love my mom did for them as well. Turns out she served her team at work and her clients the same way she served her family. We often think that great leadership is about big visions, big goals, big actions, and big success. But I learned from my mom that real leadership is about serving others by doing the little things with a big dose of selfless love.

You don't have to be great to serve, but you have to serve to be great. To make serving a habit, it's helpful to identify your caring trademark. I believe we all have one or can create one. It's the way you serve that shows you care, and it energizes you in the process. For example, I'm not going to make you a sandwich to show I care. That's not my particular caring trademark. But I'm going to encourage you. If we meet or you reach out to me, I'll encourage you.

That's my caring trademark. My wife's caring trademark is hearing what someone is saying, especially the nuances, and knowing what will help them. Your caring trademark might be cooking, like my mom, or listening really well like my dad, or coaching kids or doing handywork for your friends and neighbors or helping with technology or driving those who need a ride. There are countless ways to serve and countless caring trademarks. The key is to find yours and serve selflessly, and you will impact greatly.

SERVE WITH A CARING TRADEMARK

88

Implement the No Complaining Rule

I didn't invent the rule. I discovered it. One day I was having lunch with Dwight Cooper, a tall, thin, mild-mannered former basketball player and coach who had spent the last 15 years building and growing a company he cofounded into one of the leading nurse staffing companies in the world. Dwight's company, PPR, was named one of *Inc.* magazine's fastest-growing companies several times, but on this day it was named one of the best companies to work for in the country and Dwight was sharing a few reasons why. Dwight told me about the No Complaining Rule. He said he had read *The Energy Bus* and realized that while energy vampires can sabotage your business and team, so can subtle negativity in the form of complaining.

Dwight compared energy vampires to a kind of topical skin cancer. They don't hide. They stand right in front of you and say, "Here I am." As a result you can easily and quickly remove them. Far more dangerous is the kind of cancer that is subtle and inside your body. It grows hidden beneath the surface, sometimes slowly, sometimes fast, but either way if not caught, it eventually spreads to the point where it can and will destroy the body. Complaining is this kind of cancer to an organization and Dwight had seen it ruin far too many. He was determined not to become another statistic, and the No Complaining Rule was born.

The rule is simple: *You are not allowed to complain unless you also offer one or two possible solutions.* Dwight explained, "We introduced the rule to everyone in the company and now share it during interviews with people who want to join our team. We let them know that if you're a complainer, this isn't the right place for you. If you want to focus on solving problems, then we'd love to have you and will surely listen to you."

I knew Dwight's idea was brilliant. Every person, team, and organization not only needs to feed the positive but must also weed the negative. The No Complaining Rule is a simple, positive way to turn negative energy into positive solutions. The goal is not to eliminate all complaining—just the mindless, chronic complaining that doesn't help anyone. And the bigger goal is to turn justified complaints into positive solutions. After all, every complaint represents an opportunity to turn something negative into a positive. We can utilize customer complaints to improve our service. Employee complaints can serve as a catalyst for innovation and new processes. Our own complaints can serve as a signal letting us know what we don't want so we can focus on what we do want. And we can use the No Complaining Rule to develop a positive culture at work.

Does it work? You bet. With one simple rule you prevent the spread of toxic negative energy and empower your team to improve, innovate, and grow. Ever since learning about the rule and writing the book *The No Complaining Rule*, I've heard from hundreds of companies, schools, and teams that have transformed their culture and team dynamic with it.

Remember, it starts with you! If you're complaining, you aren't leading. Leaders don't complain; they focus on solutions. Complaining keeps you from being your best. It causes you to be stuck where you are instead of moving where you want to be. So begin by implementing the No Complaining Rule in your own life. Don't allow yourself to complain unless you use that complaint as a catalyst to create a solution. Doing this will train your mind to focus on the positive, not the negative, and empower you to transform your situation. Where complaining causes you to get stuck in the mud, the No Complaining Rule will help you leap forward!

89

Don't Waste Your Energy on Those Who Don't Get on Your Bus

As you drive through this incredible journey called life, there will be people who don't share your optimism and belief and don't buy into your vision and mission of where you're going and why you're going there. They don't get on your bus even though you asked them to join you. Don't waste your time and energy fretting that they didn't get on your bus. This drains you of the precious energy you need to keep driving forward.

Instead of being upset, frustrated, angry, and insecure because they didn't get on your bus, realize that they weren't meant to get on your bus. If they were meant to get on it, they would have joined you. Perhaps they are meant to get on another bus with someone else. Perhaps if they got on your bus, they would alter or ruin your ride. Or maybe they aren't meant to get on right now. You might have to learn and grow on your journey, and when you do they will get on at a later time. You can't worry about them or their decision. This keeps you from your decision to move forward and making it a great ride.

Your job is to keep driving your bus towards your vision and mission, realizing that not everyone is going to get on your bus, and that's okay. Some who don't get on will surprise you. And there will be some who do get on whom you never expected would support you. Just keep driving and ask more and more people to get on your bus. If you don't waste your energy on those who don't get on your bus and you keep driving with positive energy and ask more and more people to get on, eventually you'll have a standing-room-only bus filled with those who believe in you, support you, and invite others to get on the bus with you!

This habit is most critical during the beginning of the journey. It's where you'll be tested the most and where most people fail. They invite others on their bus, people don't get on, the driver gets discouraged, and the bus stops. Remember, as you begin any journey, it's just a test. Keep driving. Don't give up. Keep asking people to get on. When you get to your final destination and arrive with a smile on your face, you'll be glad you did.

90

Never Wrestle with a Pig

Country wisdom teaches, "Never wrestle with a pig. You'll both get dirty and the pig likes it." There are many who like to get dirty. They want to bait you and get you to jump into the mud with them. The guy who cuts you off on the road and gives you the finger or pulls up next to you and wants to race. The coworker who knows exactly what to say to get you to argue with them. The rude person on the plane. The family member who always picks a fight with you. The neighbor who doesn't like you and whom no one likes. The person who's having a bad day and is taking it out on everyone, including you.

Unfortunately, there have been moments in my past when I wrestled with the pig and got dirty. I regret those moments. I wish I could go back and do things differently. I didn't like myself for getting in the mud. I let the situation get the best of me and that's why I'm sharing this. You'll never regret walking away from the pig. You'll only regret getting in the mud with them.

Don't wrestle with the pig! It's not in your best interest to do this and you risk hurting yourself. Don't waste your time and energy. It's not worth it; you have better things to do. It's not your job to right their wrong. Don't get into the mud and get dirty. Don't let the person or moment get the best of you. Rise above it. Walk away from the pig. The moment will pass. The anger will subside. You'll feel better and walk away clean.

91

Take a Leap of Faith

I looked out into the Atlantic Ocean on New Year's Day with fear in my heart and uncertainty in my life. I had been fired from a dot-com company two weeks earlier with only two weeks of severance, no insurance for my two young children, and only two months of savings in the bank. My wife and I had just invested every dollar we had and even took out a second mortgage on our home and $20,000 on a credit card to open what would be the first Moe's Southwest Grill in Florida.

The restaurant was set to open January 13, and we had no earthly idea how we would pay our home mortgage and other bills, because I had planned on keeping my salary and job while my managers built the restaurant business. Now it was New Year's Day and I had no job, no salary, and a restaurant opening that at worst would fail miserably or at best take a year to be profitable.

I thought of all this as I prepared to jump into the icy cold water, to take a symbolic plunge that this would be the year of *no fear*. Regardless of the circumstances I was facing, this would be the year where I would trust and go for it. This would be the year I would be bold in actions and faith. No longer could I do it alone. Now I needed a miracle, and I decided to act as if my future depended on me and pray like it depended on God.

By jumping into the ocean, I was declaring that no longer would I allow fear to cut off the flow of abundant and positive energy in my life. No longer would I allow fear to paralyze me. Instead of fear, I would trust.

Now, many years later, I still jump into the ocean every New Year's Day. It has become my yearly ritual—to remind myself to follow my passion, live life to the fullest, surrender, and stay one step ahead of the fear that hovers around me.

And as I take my leap into the ocean, I want to invite you to jump in with me each day. Perhaps not in the ocean but in the depths of your mind. This jump doesn't necessarily require water but rather a leap of faith in your belief system and a shift in your mindset. The antidote to fear is trust, and it's only a thought away.

No one is going to push you over the chasm of struggle to the life that you want. God will nudge you, but you must take the leap. You must make this jump in your mind and then with your actions. You must make this jump with trust, determination, and faith.

After all, they don't call it a leap of fear. They call it a leap of faith for a reason. You will always feel fear. Everyone will. But your trust must be bigger than your fear. The bigger your trust, the smaller your fear becomes. And the more you trust, the more you become a conduit for miracles. I know. A consulting project presented itself out of the blue and we were able to pay our mortgage. A check came in the mail, the right opportunities came our way, and somehow, some way my family and I were carried. A year after the restaurant opened, I started writing, which eventually led to me writing many books, speaking, and doing the work I do now.

I believe each day represents a fresh start and presents a new opportunity to create the life and career you want. Each morning, decide to take a leap of faith and jump into the ocean of possibilities with all that you are and all that you wish to become!

92

Leave It Better Than You Found It

There's a company in St. Louis where every leader and team member is expected to wipe down the inside and outside of the sink in the bathroom after they're done using it. They believe in the principle and habit of leaving people and places better than you found it. It's also a great lesson and habit to live an exceptional life. Wherever you go and whatever you do, leave people, places, events, meetings, conversations, and situations better than you found them.

There are some who create conflict instead of contributing. They don't make people, places, or situations better. They make them worse. They're like a tornado wrecking everything in its path. They cause destruction and then leave, letting everyone scramble to pick up the pieces. You don't want to be the tornado. You want to be the person who calms the storm, helps clear the debris, cleans the mess, heals the pain, builds the foundation, strengthens resolve, reinforces what's possible, encourages people, and makes everyone and everything better.

How do you leave it better than you found it? Make your bed. Clean the dishes when you're done eating. Wipe down the sink. Clean the locker room. Clean up the popcorn you dropped in the theater. Put away your cart at the grocery store. Tip the driver. Add value in the meeting. Encourage your friend who is struggling. Coach others and make them better. Lead by example. Work hard. Give your best! Share a good idea in the conversation. Heal instead of divide. Love instead of hate. Believe in people. See the good in them. Landscape a yard. Build a water well where they don't have running water. Clean up your local park. Transform the culture in your school. Do team building with your team. Refurbish a home. Train people at the gym. Speak life into a kid. Tell someone they matter. Share health tips on social media. Implement the habits in this book.

The ways you can leave it better than you found it are endless. The question is, will you intentionally make them a habit? When you do, you'll be the person others trust, count on, thank, remember, appreciate, and call. Those who want to get better want to be around and work with those who make them and their situation better.

93

The Final Habit: Create an Amazing Funeral

Stephen Covey taught us to live with the end in mind in his iconic book *The 7 Habits of Highly Effective People*. This habit is about starting with a clear understanding of your destination. You need to know where you're going in order to take the necessary steps to get there. It's about envisioning the ideal outcome you want and aligning your actions and habits to bring about this outcome.

That's why when people ask me about the vision I have for my life, it's to create an amazing funeral. Because in my mind, when your life ends on earth and there is a funeral for you, the kind of funeral held for you says everything about how you lived and the life and relationships you created.

Some might consider it morbid to think about your own funeral, but this is the ultimate example of living with the end in mind. Knowing how you want to be remembered at the end helps you decide how to live today. This brings clarity, focus, and intention to your life and causes you think about and do what matters most. If you want an amazing funeral, you're going to live in such a way that brings about this outcome as you reach your destination.

"But you won't be there to enjoy it," some people have said to me. That's true, but an amazing funeral will mean I enjoyed my life and took the time to help others and showed them I cared about them and impacted their life in a meaningful way. While it wouldn't benefit me if they came to my funeral, it would mean that I benefited them during my life.

When I think about my amazing funeral, I envision a lot of people celebrating, not because I died (that wouldn't be good!) but because I truly lived. I see wonderful people grateful that I wrote books and encouraged them. I see them meeting each other and telling stories. I see people talking to my kids and telling them how something I wrote or said during a talk impacted their life, work, or family. I see younger people I have spoken to on the phone when they were struggling teenagers now older with families. They were going to give up but they didn't because of our conversation. They were going down the wrong path but they changed course and created an amazing life.

This vision I have for my amazing funeral guides me each day. It reminds me to make time for people. To help those I'm supposed to help. To be a better leader, husband, and father. To give to those in need. To create great memories. To write when I don't feel like it. To give my all in a talk because there is someone there who needs to hear something I'm meant to say. To do what matters most and live life to the fullest. My goal is not to be the richest man on earth. It's to create an amazing funeral, and if I do this, I'll be the richest man in Heaven! Rich with love. Rich with relationships. Rich with impact!

I hope this encourages you more than it scares you. I hope this helps you decide to live with the actual end in mind. I hope this final habit helps you live a life filled with many of the habits in this book. And I hope these habits lead to an amazing celebration at the end of your life where everyone is celebrating you because you lived, touched their life, and put your fingerprints on their soul.

The best is yet to come and I am rooting for you!

ACCESS EXCLUSIVE POWER OF POSITIVE HABITS RESOURCES

Including:

- **Positive Habits Developer** - An interactive tool where you plug in your habits and receive a personalized 30-day custom habit plan built specifically for YOU.

- **Workbook / Action Plan Accompaniment** - Turn ideas from the book into actions and results.

And more!

Go to →

 www.PowerOfPositiveHabitsBook.com/Resources

BE MENTORED BY JON AND HIS TEAM

Get the support, strategies, and tools you need to thrive as a confident Leader.

Certified Positive Leader is a monthly live masterclass (1 hour a month) that gives you the confidence, accessible leadership tools, support and community to strengthen your mindset, elevate your leadership and build a team that delivers results. If you want to grow as a leader, this is for you.

**ENERGIZE YOUR LEADERSHIP...
BECOME A CERTIFIED POSITIVE LEADER!**

www.JonGordon.com/CPL

BRING THE POWER OF POSITIVE LEADERSHIP TO YOUR ORGANIZATION

» **Keynotes and Workshops** - Our keynotes and workshops are designed to help you and your team achieve exceptional results. Visit www.JonGordon.com or call 904-285-6842

» **Action Plans** - Turn ideas from the book into actions and results. Visit www.Jongordon.com/ActionPlans

» **Train Positive Leaders in Your Organization** - We provide you with facilitator guides, workbooks, PowerPoints, hand-outs and everything you need to train and develop positive leaders in your organization. Visit www.JonGordonCertified.com to learn more.

Other Books by Jon Gordon

The Energy Bus

A man whose life and career are in shambles learns from a unique bus driver and set of passengers how to overcome adversity. Enjoy an enlightening ride of positive energy that is improving the way leaders lead, employees work, and teams function.
www.TheEnergyBus.com

The Energy Bus Field Guide

Jon Gordon's international bestseller, *The Energy Bus*, has inspired thousands of businesses, organizations, sport teams, schools, and families alike, helping them cultivate positive energy, overcome adversity, and bring out the best in themselves and those around them. *The Energy Bus Field Guide* is a simple and powerful guide for putting *The Energy Bus* lessons to work. Using the 10 principles, you'll discover how to navigate the twists and turns that often sabotage individual and team success, and how to move in the right direction with vision, focus, purpose, and positive energy.

The Energy Bus for Schools

Based on *The Energy Bus*, the *Wall Street Journal* bestseller by lead author Jon Gordon, *The Energy Bus for Schools* teaches educators how to fuel their schools, themselves, and their students with positive energy. Research shows that culture and leadership greatly influence a school's learning environment and students' academic success. This book will help teachers work together to create a school culture where school leaders and students can grow into positive leaders, energizing their school culture as a united front.

The Energy Bus for Schools Field Guide

The Energy Bus for Schools Field Guide delivers an easy-to-use roadmap for transforming the insights found in the companion book, *The Energy Bus for Schools,* into effective and powerful solutions for schools everywhere.

The No Complaining Rule

Follow a vice president of human resources who must save herself and her company from ruin and discover proven principles and an actionable plan to win the battle against individual and organizational negativity.
www.NoComplainingRule.com

Training Camp

This inspirational story about a small guy with a big heart, and a special coach who guides him on a quest for excellence, reveals the 11 winning habits that separate the best individuals and teams from the rest.
www.TrainingCamp11.com

The Shark and the Goldfish

Delightfully illustrated, this quick read is packed with tips and strategies on how to respond to challenges beyond your control in order to thrive during waves of change.
www.SharkandGoldfish.com

Soup

The newly appointed CEO of a popular soup company is brought in to reinvigorate the brand and bring success back to a company that has fallen on hard times. Through her journey, discover the key ingredients to unite, engage, and inspire teams to create a culture of greatness.
www.Soup11.com

Other Books by Jon Gordon

The Seed

Go on a quest for the meaning and passion behind work with Josh, an up-and-comer at his company who is disenchanted with his job. Through Josh's cross-country journey, you'll find surprising new sources of wisdom and inspiration in your own business and life.
www.Seed11.com

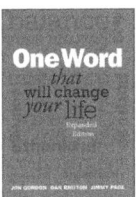

One Word

One Word is a simple concept that delivers powerful life change! This quick read will inspire you to simplify your life and work by focusing on just one word for this year. *One Word* creates clarity, power, passion, and life-change. When you find your word, live it, and share it, your life will become more rewarding and exciting than ever.
www.getoneword.com

The Positive Dog

We all have two dogs inside of us. One dog is positive, happy, optimistic, and hopeful. The other dog is negative, mad, pessimistic, and fearful. These two dogs often fight inside us, but guess who wins? The one you feed the most. *The Positive Dog* is an inspiring story that not only reveals the strategies and benefits of being positive, but also an essential truth: Being positive doesn't just make you better; it makes everyone around you better.
www.feedthepositivedog.com

Other Books by Jon Gordon

The Carpenter

The Carpenter is Jon Gordon's most inspiring book yet—filled with powerful lessons and success strategies. Michael wakes up in the hospital with a bandage on his head and fear in his heart after collapsing during a morning jog. When Michael finds out the man who saved his life is a carpenter, he visits him and quickly learns that he is more than just a carpenter; he is also a builder of lives, careers, people, and teams. In this journey, you will learn timeless principles to help you stand out, excel, and make an impact on people and the world.
www.carpenter11.com

The Hard Hat

A true story about Cornell lacrosse player George Boiardi, *The Hard Hat* is an unforgettable book about a selfless, loyal, joyful, hard-working, competitive, and compassionate leader and teammate, the impact he had on his team and program, and the lessons we can learn from him. This inspirational story will teach you how to build a great team and be the best teammate you can be.
www.hardhat21.com

You Win in the Locker Room First

Based on the extraordinary experiences of NFL Coach Mike Smith and leadership expert Jon Gordon, *You Win in the Locker Room First* offers a rare, behind-the-scenes look at one of the most pressure-packed leadership jobs on the planet, and what leaders can learn from these experiences in order to build their own winning teams.
www.wininthelockerroom.com

Other Books by Jon Gordon

Life Word

Life Word reveals a simple, powerful tool to help you identify the word that will inspire you to live your best life while leaving your greatest legacy. In the process, you'll discover your *why*, which will help show you how to live with a renewed sense of power, purpose, and passion.
www.getoneword.com/lifeword

The Power of Positive Leadership

The Power of Positive Leadership returns in this expanded Second Edition as a clear, practical guide to becoming the leader your team deserves. Drawing on lessons from Jon Gordon's bestselling fables and real-world experience, this edition highlights the essential principles that drive positive leadership. In challenging times, results grow from culture, teamwork, vision, innovation, and commitment. This book shows you how to strengthen these foundations and lead with clarity, purpose, and lasting impact.
www.powerofpositiveleadership.com

The Power of a Positive Team

In *The Power of a Positive Team*, Jon Gordon draws on his unique team-building experience, as well as conversations with some of the greatest teams in history, to provide an essential framework of proven practices to empower teams to work together more effectively and achieve superior results.
www.PowerOfAPositiveTeam.com

The Coffee Bean

From bestselling author Jon Gordon and rising star Damon West comes *The Coffee Bean*: an illustrated fable that teaches readers how to transform their environment, overcome challenges, and create positive change.
www.coffeebeanbook.com

Other Books by Jon Gordon

Stay Positive

Fuel yourself and others with positive energy—inspirational quotes and encouraging messages to live by from bestselling author Jon Gordon. Keep this little book by your side, read from it each day, and feed your mind, body, and soul with the power of positivity.
www.StayPositiveBook.com

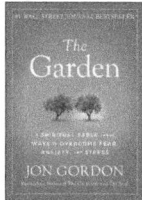
The Garden

The Garden is an enlightening and encouraging fable that helps readers overcome the 5 D's (doubt, distortion, discouragement, distractions, and division) in order to find more peace, focus, connection, and happiness. Jon tells a story of teenage twins who, through the help of a neighbor and his special garden, find ancient wisdom, life-changing lessons, and practical strategies to overcome the fear, anxiety, and stress in their lives.
www.readthegarden.com

Relationship Grit

Bestselling author Jon Gordon is back with another life-affirming book. This time, he teams up with Kathryn Gordon, his wife of 23 years, for a look at what it takes to build strong relationships. In *Relationship Grit*, the Gordons reveal what brought them together, what kept them together through difficult times, and what continues to sustain their love and passion for one another to this day.
www.relationshipgritbook.com

Stick Together

From bestselling author Jon Gordon and coauthor Kate Leavell, *Stick Together* delivers a crucial message about the power of belief, ownership, connection, love, inclusion, consistency, and hope. The authors guide individuals and teams on an inspiring journey to show them how to persevere through challenges, overcome obstacles, and create success together.
www.sticktogetherbook.com

Other Books by Jon Gordon

Row the Boat

In *Row the Boat*, Minnesota Golden Gophers Head Coach P.J. Fleck and bestselling author Jon Gordon deliver an inspiring message about what you can achieve when you approach life with a never-give-up philosophy. The book shows you how to choose enthusiasm and optimism as your guiding lights instead of being defined by circumstances and events outside of your control.
www.rowtheboatbook.com

The Sale

In *The Sale*, bestselling author Jon Gordon and rising star Alex Demczak deliver an invaluable lesson about what matters most in life and work and how to achieve it. The book teaches four lessons about integrity in order to create lasting success.
www.thesalebook.com

The One Word Journal

In *The One Word Journal*, bestselling authors Jon Gordon, Dan Britton, and Jimmy Page deliver a powerful new approach to simplifying and transforming your life and business. You'll learn how to access the core of your intention every week of the year as you explore 52 weekly lessons, principles, and wins that unleash the power of your One Word.

How to Be a Coffee Bean

In *How to Be a Coffee Bean*, bestselling coauthors of *The Coffee Bean*, Jon Gordon and Damon West, present 111 simple and effective strategies to help you lead a coffee bean lifestyle—one full of healthy habits, encouragement, and genuine happiness. From athletes to students and executives, countless individuals have been inspired by *The Coffee Bean* message. Now, *How to Be a Coffee Bean* teaches you how to put *The Coffee Bean* philosophy into action to help you create real and lasting change in your life.

Other Books by Jon Gordon

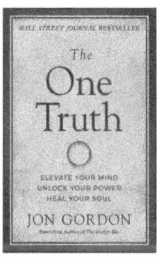

The One Truth

In *The One Truth*, bestselling author and thought leader Jon Gordon guides you on a path to discover revolutionary insights, ancient truths, and practical strategies to elevate your mind, unlock your power, and live life to the fullest. Once you know the One Truth, you'll see how it impacts leadership, teamwork, mindset, performance, relationships, addictions, social media, anxiety, mental health, healing, and ultimately determines what you create and experience.

Success Journal

Success Journal: A Daily Practice for Positivity, Resilience, and Growth is a daily, lined journal where readers can write down their success of the day, shift their nighttime focus from negativity to positivity, and thereby create more success and opportunities in their lives. This resource is inspired by the legendary Bart Conner, who credited his overcoming a torn bicep muscle to win two gold medals at the 1984 Olympics to his parents asking him about his success of the day as a child.

The Energy Bus for Kids

The illustrated children's adaptation of the bestselling book *The Energy Bus* tells the story of George, who, with the help of his school bus driver, Joy, learns that if he believes in himself, he'll find the strength to overcome any challenge. His journey teaches kids how to overcome negativity, bullies, and everyday challenges to be their best.
www.EnergyBusKids.com

Thank You and Good Night

Thank You and Good Night is a beautifully illustrated book that shares the heart of gratitude. Jon Gordon takes a little boy and girl on a fun-filled journey from one perfect moonlit night to the next. During their adventurous days and nights, the children explore the people, places, and things they are thankful for.

Other Books by Jon Gordon

The Hard Hat for Kids

The Hard Hat for Kids is an illustrated guide to teamwork. Adapted from the bestseller *The Hard Hat*, this uplifting story presents practical insights and life-changing lessons that are immediately applicable to everyday situations, giving kids—and adults—a new outlook on cooperation, friendship, and the selfless nature of true teamwork.
www.HardHatforKids.com

One Word for Kids

If you could choose only one word to help you have your best year ever, what would it be? *Love? Fun? Believe? Brave?* It's probably different for each person. How you find your word is just as important as the word itself. And once you know your word, what do you do with it? In *One Word for Kids,* bestselling author Jon Gordon—along with coauthors Dan Britton and Jimmy Page—asks these questions to children and adults of all ages, teaching an important life lesson in the process.
www.getoneword.com/kids

The Coffee Bean for Kids

The bestselling authors of *The Coffee Bean* inspire and encourage children with this transformative tale of personal strength. Perfect for parents, teachers, and children who wish to overcome negativity and challenging situations, *The Coffee Bean for Kids* teaches readers about the potential that each one of us has to lead, influence, and make a positive impact on others and the world.
www.coffeebeankidsbook.com

Other Books by Jon Gordon